READING JUDAS

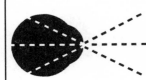

This Large Print Book carries the
Seal of Approval of N.A.V.H.

READING JUDAS

THE GOSPEL OF JUDAS AND THE SHAPING OF CHRISTIANITY

ELAINE PAGELS AND KAREN L. KING

WHEELER PUBLISHING
A part of Gale, Cengage Learning

GALE
CENGAGE Learning

Detroit • New York • San Francisco • New Haven, Conn • Waterville, Maine • London

GALE
CENGAGE Learning

LIBRARY OF CONGRESS CATALOGING-IN-PUBLICATION DATA

Pagels, Elaine H., 1943–
    Reading Judas : the Gospel of Judas and the shaping of
Christianity / by Elaine Pagels and Karen L. King.
      p. cm.
    Includes bibliographical references.
    ISBN-13: 978-1-59722-717-9 (lg. print : alk. paper)
    ISBN-10: 1-59722-717-X (lg. print : alk. paper)
    1. Gospel of Judas — Criticism, interpretation, etc. 2. Large
type books. I. King, Karen L., 1954– II. Title.
BS2860.J832P34 2008
229'.8—dc22   2007046860

Published in 2008 by arrangement with Viking, a member of Penguin
Group (USA) Inc.

To Lyn and Norman Lear
in loving friendship
— *E. P.*
and
To Norman C. Cluley
with warmest gratitude
for his unfailing love and support
— *K. L. K.*

CONTENTS

INTRODUCTION

For more than a decade we had heard rumors that a fabled gospel ascribed to Judas Iscariot had been discovered. In April 2006, the archaeological find was at last made public by the National Geographic Society. We now know that sometime in the 1970s, a copy of the *Gospel of Judas,* translated into Coptic from its original second-century Greek, had been found in Middle Egypt near Al Minya. It is rumored that peasants accidentally came upon a burial cave containing a limestone box that for centuries had carefully preserved ancient writings. One of these was a papyrus book (the Tchacos Codex) that dates approximately to the fourth century. Over the years, dealers secretly showed these writings to a number of people in efforts to sell them at an extraordinary price. Moved from place to place and improperly stored — first in a humid safety-deposit box in Hicksville, New

York, for almost seventeen years, and later frozen (!) — the Tchacos Codex suffered considerable damage from the time it was found until 2001, when it came into the able hands of the philologian Rodolphe Kasser, who, along with the conservator Florence Darbre and the historian Gregor Wurst, labored hard over the fragments for five years to restore the text as close as possible to its original condition. The new translation into English offered here is based on their work.[1]

Our concern here, however, is not with the history of the discovery but with the meaning of this extraordinary find. Historians already knew about the *Gospel of Judas* from the writing *Against Heresies* by the second-century church father Irenaeus, who wrote about a group of Christians:

> They declare that Judas the traitor was thoroughly acquainted with these things, and that he alone, knowing the truth as no others did, accomplished the mystery of the betrayal; by him all things, both earthly and heavenly, were thus thrown into confusion. They produced a fictitious history of this kind, which they style the Gospel of Judas.[2]

The *Gospel of Judas* thus must have existed at the time Irenaeus wrote against it, around 180 C.E. The gospel itself was probably written in the mid–second century — but Irenaeus's comments only provoke more questions. What did this mysterious gospel say beyond promoting Judas as the one "who knew the truth as no others did"? What truth did he know?

At our first reading, the author of the *Gospel of Judas* struck us as a very angry man with an offensive, even hateful, message, for he portrays Jesus repeatedly mocking his disciples and charging them with committing all kinds of sins and impurities in his name. And it seemed to us that the author was doing exactly that himself — using Jesus's name to propagate his own homophobic and anti-Jewish views. We felt an immediate aversion to the *Gospel's* sometimes strident, mocking tone and slanderous accusations. It felt too much like the other side of the bitter invective so well known from the harangues of early church fathers like Irenaeus against their opponents — the kind of polarizing language that is so deeply disturbing in our own era of religious and political discord and violence.

But once we moved past this initial impression, we found that not all is angry.

Much of the *Gospel of Judas* is filled with Jesus's brilliant teaching about the spiritual life. Why, then, the author's rage? What matters so deeply? And most important, what hope does the author offer to redeem his anger? The answers to these questions lead deep into the agonizing controversies and exultant visions of God that would ultimately come to shape Christianity and capture the hearts and souls of people for millennia to come. These are the matters we address in *Reading Judas: The Gospel of Judas and the Shaping of Christianity.*

The most obvious questions are the easiest to answer: Did Judas really write this gospel? Can we learn anything new here about the historical Judas, Jesus, or his other disciples? Because the *Gospel of Judas* was written sometime around 150 C.E., about a century after Judas would have lived, it is impossible that he wrote it; the real author remains anonymous. Neither do we learn anything historically reliable about Judas or Jesus beyond what we already know from other early Christian literature. Instead, the *Gospel of Judas* opens a window onto the disputes among second-century Christians over the meaning of Judas's betrayal and Jesus's teaching, raising such questions as: Why would a troubled disciple betray his master, Jesus? How could any Christian imagine Judas — his betrayer — to be Jesus's favorite and most trusted disciple? Why condemn Jesus's other disciples as immoral killers? What are "the mysteries of the kingdom" that Jesus reveals to Judas alone? Why is it his star that leads the way?

To understand what inspires the author's passion, we have to place the people who wrote and read the *Gospel of Judas* in the midst of the controversies and visions that shaped it. Some scholars have tried to do this by categorizing the *Gospel of Judas* as a "Gnostic" gospel, placing it on the losing side of battles waged among early Christians with diverse interpretations, beliefs, and practices, each group claiming to be the only one with the truth (the "orthodox"). And indeed the *Gospel of Judas* in some respects resembles other early Christian works that have been discovered in Egypt over the last century and that scholars label "Gnostic," especially those from the remarkable find near the village of Nag Hammadi in Egypt in 1945.[3] Many of those texts, too, let us hear voices that have been lost for over fifteen hundred years, silenced by those who won the name of orthodoxy for themselves.

Like some of these other newly recovered

13

works, the *Gospel of Judas* understands human nature to be essentially spiritual, believing that the physical body decomposes at death while the spirit-filled soul lives forever with God in a heavenly world above. It, too, sees Jesus as the divine revealer sent by God to teach about his kingdom to an ignorant and unrighteous — or self-righteous — humanity.

But calling the text Gnostic can also lead to a number of false impressions, primarily because until recently, scholars have derived their descriptions of "Gnostic" Christians almost solely from the early church fathers, not from the newly discovered writings. Indeed, they invented the term *Gnosticism* in the eighteenth century, long before the new texts were discovered. The only primary sources available to historians then were from those Christians like Irenaeus, who had written *against* works like the *Gospel of Judas.* So modern scholars' views are defined by their characterizations of heresy. As a result, we continue to hear only one side of the debates — the view of the winners — making it almost impossible to imagine what Christianity was like at the time the *Gospel of Judas* was written, when Christianity was developing and it was not clear whose views would dominate.

An even more difficult problem is that reading the new texts through the lenses of their opponents distorts what the *Gospel of Judas* and other newly discovered texts are saying, and makes it hard to see what the passionate arguments that informed them were really about.[4] Reading the *Gospel of Judas* as just another example of well-known Gnostic heresy merely repeats entrenched clichés, for we only hear the losers' voices yet again. But if we can get beyond the stereotypes that come from hearing only one side of the story — a version told so often and for so long that it has wrongly come to seem like the only possible story — then these new finds can enrich our knowledge of the diversity of early Christian imagination and practice, letting us read both the new discoveries and well-known tradition with new eyes. When we do, we can see now that the burning issue in the *Gospel of Judas* was one that the church fathers took pains to avoid addressing by diverting attention to other concerns.

As we will see, what roused such anger was the agonizing deaths of fellow Christians at the hands of the Romans.[5] The author of the *Gospel of Judas* could not reconcile his belief in a deeply loving, good God with a particular idea other Christians held at the time: that God desired the bloody sacrificial death of Jesus and his followers. In this author's view, Christian leaders who called on their fellow Christians to "glorify" themselves that way were murderers. They had totally misunderstood Jesus's teaching and were worshipping a false god. Judas alone among the disciples understood Jesus's teaching and that was why he handed him over to be killed. In the end, the *Gospel of Judas* shows us how some Christians were struggling with issues of suffering and death that concern us all, and how they envisioned a spiritual connection with God that persists now and forever.

Identifying Judas as Jesus's most loyal confidant was no accident. Whoever wrote the *Gospel of Judas* was well aware that Christians almost uniformly condemned Judas as a betrayer; the author even has Jesus tell Judas that he will be cursed by the rest of humanity (*Judas* 9:28). Indeed, the author must have chosen Judas precisely in order to shock other Christians of his own day.[6] When he accused them of human sacrifice, false worship, and other despicable heresy, his tone is not one of gentle persuasion or peaceful discussion: It is a direct and sustained attack on the deeply held convictions of certain other Christians.

Not all disagreements among Christians divided them, but those expressed in the *Gospel of Judas* surely did. For the author of this gospel has Jesus tell his disciples that in the end God will condemn them and they will be destroyed (5:16; 14:16) — except for Judas, who will rule over them all (9:29). He is the prophet of the end times, and Jesus tells him, "Already your horn is raised up and your anger is full, your star has passed by and your heart has prevailed" (15:5).

The author of the *Gospel of Judas* speaks as "true believers" so often do — insisting that only those who stand with him will prevail — and that God will utterly condemn everyone else. Like sectarians from his own time to the present, this author insists on breaking away from everyone else to form the only "pure" group of "true Christians" — just as he pictures Jesus telling Judas *twice* that he must separate himself from the others. Separating the other disciples is a judgment against them — but one which hints that those behind the *Gospel of Judas* are on the defensive. Its author hurls charges so outrageous that they cannot be taken literally — but they do show how hot feelings were running during a climate of persecution, when all Christians must have felt themselves in danger of arrest and execution. Meanwhile, leaders like Tertullian were accusing people who avoided martyrdom by fleeing of being cowards with only a frivolous and cold faith, people who would end up in hell along with all who followed them.[7]

This author could object, however, that neither Jesus nor Judas avoided violent death. Judas actually becomes the first martyr, for according to the *Gospel of Judas,* he did not commit suicide but was stoned to death by "the twelve" (*Judas* 9:7–8). By charging Christians with Judas's death, the *Gospel of Judas* throws the bishops and their followers together with Roman persecutors, whom he accuses of worshipping demons. All of this suggests that the anguish on both sides of the dispute has erupted into uncontrolled bitterness. It is impossible to imagine them gathering to worship together in the same community of Christian fellowship and love.

Yet the *Gospel of Judas,* even in its fragmentary state, shows us far more than a glimpse into one particular dispute. It also offers a window onto the complex world of the early Christian movement and shows us that what later historians depicted as an unbroken procession of a uniform faith was nothing of the kind. As we said, the traditional history of Christianity is written almost solely from the viewpoint of the side that won, which was remarkably successful in silencing or distorting other voices, destroying their writings, and suppressing any who disagreed with them as dangerous and obstinate "heretics." In place of the intense controversies and startling innovations from which the movement was born, they pictured Jesus teaching his simple gospel to "the twelve," who, in turn, handed down the same exact message — which they called the "deposit of faith," like money deposited in a bank. With fixed creed and canon, the disciples' followers then supposedly delivered the message intact to the next generations of proper guardians of divine truth — to bishops and other ordained clergy all over the world. Many people have found this picture enormously appealing because it assures them that what they have learned as "Christianity" must be God's truth. That picture of early Christian history could remain unquestioned only so long as the voices of dissent were absent.

But whoever reflects on how revolutions actually happen — including religious revolutions — realizes that this picture not only distorts the historical account by freezing its vibrant dynamism but that the picture is also a hugely oversimplified one. Over the last 150 years or so, we have gained access to over forty gospels, letters, and other early Christian works.[8] We can now see more clearly that the early history of Christianity was tumultuous — a time of intense reflection, experimentation, and struggle involving every fundamental issue.

But, someone may ask, are these "other voices" really *Christian?* We often use the term as if its definition were clear, fixed, and universal, and speak as if it were obvious what is Christian; but in the second century, as in the twenty-first, those on both sides of various controversies often claimed to possess the truth for themselves — and denied that claim to others. In the same way, historians often used to speak of "*the* early Christian church" — as if only one group met in each city and every member was united with every other one by the same teaching, ritual practices, and concerns for the poor and sick. Historians today, however, see that major cities would have had many groups of Jesus's followers. Just as varied groups can be found in any cosmopolitan center today, from New York to Mexico City, from Johannesburg to Brussels, so during the second century in the city of Rome, for example, churches formed of believers who came from all over the empire — from Syria and Turkey, Egypt and North Africa. They spoke Greek and Latin or tongues from their native lands; many were bilingual. Some of the immigrants were prominent teachers, offering instruction in the "philosophy" of Christianity — and often sparking deep controversy among themselves and their students.[9] We now can see that what used to be called "*the* Christian Church" at Rome, as if there were only one, actually consisted of an aggregate of groups located in different sections of the city. Each group was its own island, with its own meeting place, its own leaders, and very often its own understanding of the gospel. Although various groups may have perceived themselves as "cells of one church" and sometimes worked together, for example in collecting for the poor or sharing eucharist gifts, no unified or uniform institution existed. Only in the second half of the second century do we see a single bishop elevated over the rest — and with that, clear lines start to be drawn, dividing the groups by excluding those now regarded as "heretics." This is the story for second-century Rome. No doubt the situation in other cities varied, but the result was the same.

The rise of bishops, however, did not eliminate the competition or end the controversy. As the movement attracted increasing numbers of new members, it simultaneously attracted intense suspicion from hostile outsiders, and stories of persecution and martyrdom became increasingly widespread. Teachers like the second-century martyr Justin tried to defend Christians from hostile charges while at the same time attacking other Christians, even respected leaders like the Egyptian poet and spiritual director Valentinus, calling them "heretics," accusing members of such groups of being inspired by Satan. Irenaeus, who became a bishop in rural Gaul, traveled to Rome to visit a bishop there and was distressed and shocked by the diversity he found among Christian groups in Rome. Following Justin's example, Irenaeus sought to create a unified church by denouncing independent spiritual teachers, insisting that everyone must believe the same doctrines and consigning all gospels other than the canonical four to the rubbish heap. About 150 years later, the most unexpected convert of all, Constantine, who became emperor of the Roman empire — with Christ's help, he

believed — answered the prayers of persecuted believers by stopping the persecution
and becoming instead the defender and
patron of Christians throughout the Roman
world. But being a pragmatic ruler, Constantine attempted to resolve the differences
among various Christians by supporting
certain powerful leaders — men who were
bishops of churches in major areas. Constantine funded only groups that agreed to
a definition of Christianity, which was
established by bishops he gathered together
in 325 C.E. at the lakeside town of Nicaea
in present-day Turkey. Those who objected
were cursed ("anathematized"). In the following centuries, dissenters saw their build-
ings confiscated or burned to the ground,
and their members either forced to conform
with Nicene teaching and practice or
hounded out of the churches as "heretics."
Although their many writings had been read
and copied for centuries, those too were —
quite literally — forced underground, mute
casualties of the war against heresy.

Yet not everything was lost. Like the *Gospel of Judas,* many books were buried in jars
or hidden in graves, preserved for a distant
future in which their silenced voices might
speak again. Before these writings were
recovered, it was hard for us to read the

ancient accounts of Irenaeus and others who ridiculed these texts and understand why anyone would take the time and effort to bother to refute such preposterous and immoral ideas. But now that these lost Christians speak in their own voices, we are learning why they were such a threat to other Christians and why the attacks were so agonizing. We can see that they raised deep and compelling issues — about the nature of God, the meaning of Jesus's teaching, the suffering of martyrs, and much else — issues close to those in our own day.

The *Gospel of Judas,* as no other surviving work from earliest Christianity, exposes the agonizing passion and the anger some Christians felt at the horrible, violent deaths of their family and friends — fellow believers who were put to death to entertain the Roman crowds and to cower any resistance into submission. But their anger was directed less against the Romans than at their own leaders for encouraging Christians to accept martyrdom as God's will, as though God desired these tortured bodies for his own glory. We can feel their visceral denial that such a God was worthy of any honor. The *Gospel of Judas* shows us that the God they worshipped — and the religion they were ready to die for — was different. Jesus

24

taught about the mysteries of the kingdom, about the realm of the luminous God beyond this world of chaos and death, the God who had prepared an eternal home in a great house made of living greenery and light above. As the age of martyrdom closed with the conversion of Constantine, stories glorifying the martyrs came to dominate the history of Christian origins, providing spiritual heroes for the new imperial church. The *Gospel of Judas* restores to us one voice of dissent, a call for religion to renounce violence as God's will and purpose for humanity.

However we evaluate these new voices, their existence means that it will no longer be possible to tell the story of Christianity the same way. Gospels we had never known now invite us to enter the extraordinarily dynamic world in which Christianity was shaped. They offer us the opportunity — and the challenge — to see with new eyes the familiar traditions we call Christianity.

■ ■ ■ ■

PART ONE:
READING JUDAS

■ ■ ■ ■

CHAPTER ONE:
JUDAS: BETRAYER OR FAVORED DISCIPLE?

What would so trouble a loyal disciple, after a long and arduous time devoted to his teacher, that he would betray him to the enemies who for years had wanted to kill him? Why would Judas have identified Jesus to the armed crowd of men who came to capture and arrest him late at night, when most of those who would defend him were sleeping?

For thousands of years, Christians have pictured Judas as the incarnation of evil. Motivated by greed and inspired by Satan, he is the betrayer whom Dante placed in the lowest circle of hell. But the *Gospel of Judas* shows Judas instead as Jesus's closest and most trusted confidant — the one to whom Jesus reveals his deepest mysteries and whom he trusts to initiate the passion. Startling as this sounds at first, the perceptive reader will note that the familiar New Testament gospels have long offered hints of this. All the New Testament gospel writers agree that Jesus anticipated, even embraced, his own death. The *Gospel of Mark* says that right before Jesus led his followers toward Jerusalem, where he would suffer and die, he secretly told them that it was necessary for all these things to happen (*Mark* 8:31). The *Gospel of John* suggests that Jesus himself was complicit in the betrayal, that moments before Judas went out, Jesus had told him, "Do quickly what you are going to do" (*John* 13:27).[1] The *Gospel of Judas* follows these hints to their logical conclusion. And yet it, too, does not resolve the issue finally but only succeeds in raising again — and more forcefully than ever — the question of why Jesus was betrayed and what his death means.

The New Testament gospels show that after Jesus's shocking arrest, torture, and slow, horrifying public execution, various groups of his followers told and retold those events as they struggled to understand how things could have gone so wrong. If Jesus had been God's chosen one, how could his enemies have gained power to kill him? Who actually engineered the plot that succeeded? What role did Judas really play? Despite all that the New Testament gospels say, the various anecdotes about Judas left many questions open — questions that have baffled and intrigued people ever since. The betrayer always intrigues us more than the disciples who remain loyal, as artists have shown, from Giotto's famous painting of the traitor's kiss to the paradoxical story of Judas written by Jorge Luis Borges; from Martin Scorsese's film *The Last Temptation of Christ* to Michelangelo's Satan, pictured for eternity in the act of devouring Judas in hell.

The New Testament gospels suggest that by the time Jesus entered Jerusalem for the last time, his fame as a teacher and healer had gained him a large following, a situation that aroused the Roman rulers to suspect he was fomenting revolution, and so they put him to death as a signal to other would-be rabble-rousers and rebels. And indeed his capture, arrest, and execution could have ended the story. Many quit the movement at that point. The *Gospel of Luke* tries to counter these disappointments by telling a story of two who initially had given up hope. As they explained to a traveler, "(W)e had hoped that he was the one to redeem Israel" (*Luke* 24:21), but events had proved them wrong — until Jesus himself miraculously appeared and set them straight. Yet others stubbornly held to their convictions. Rumors that close companions, like Mary of Magdala and Peter, had seen him miraculously alive again electrified some of his followers, who declared that they believed these stories, even though many others rejected them outright. But instead of clarifying everything, the resurrection stories, too, raised more questions. Why had his death been necessary? What had it accomplished?

Now, however, the *Gospel of Judas,* along with many other ancient Christian texts discovered recently, from the *Gospel of Mary of Magdala* to the *Apocalypse of Peter,* lets us see that the New Testament writers were not the only ones troubled by these questions. Various Christians among the earliest generations asked — and struggled to answer — fundamental questions that look past Judas to Jesus. Who was — or is — Jesus? And what is the "good news" (that is, the *gospel*) about him? Although these works have been lost for over fifteen hundred years, ancient accounts had told us about them. Irenaeus, bishop of Lyons, knew about such gospels and mentioned the *Gospel of Judas* among many others, including the *Gospel to the Egyptians* and the *Gospel of Thomas.* Irenaeus realized that some Christians used only *one* gospel, while others used several, along with the letters of Paul the apostle and many other writings attributed to Jesus's disciples. But Irenaeus was suspicious of those who used so many of these gospels, suggesting that those who did so were heretics; for, he declared, "the heretics say that they have more gospels than there really are . . . but in reality, they have no gospel that is not full of blasphemy."[2] Irenaeus was the first, so far as we know, to insist that the church has "only *four* gospels, not more and not fewer." Why not? Irenaeus offers a cosmological explanation. Just as "there are four corners of the universe, and four universal winds," so, he says, "it is fitting that she should have four pillars" that hold up God's truth.[3] And why *these four?* The *Gospels of Matthew* and *John,* Irenaeus declared, were written by actual apostles, and *Mark* and *Luke* by disciples of these apostles. These gospels were reliable, he argued, because they alone could be traced back to eyewitness accounts written by Jesus's most trusted followers.

Few New Testament scholars today would agree with Irenaeus's reasoning, much less with what he says about who wrote these gospels. For while the New Testament gospels contain traditions — sayings of Jesus, parables, and anecdotes — that go

33

back to early times, even the earliest of the gospels, the *Gospel of Mark,* was written about forty years after Jesus's death, and the rest about ten to thirty years later. It is highly unlikely that any of them were written by disciples who personally knew Jesus, but we do not know who actually wrote them. Furthermore, many of the gospels that Irenaeus dismisses as illegitimate, like the *Gospel of Thomas* and the *Gospel of Philip,* also claim to be written by members of the same inner circle of disciples; but we have no independent evidence to verify who actually wrote any of them, either.

The claims to apostolic authorship — whether by Irenaeus or those he opposed — belong to second-century battles over whose views would dominate the nascent Christian. religion. Certainly, those who wrote and circulated the gospels Irenaeus denounced did not think of themselves as heretics but as Christians. Now that we possess not only Irenaeus's refutation but copies of some of the works he wrote against — including the *Gospel of Judas* — we can see how one-sided his presentation is. And for the first time, we can hear other sides of the debate.[4] If we were now to put Irenaeus in conversation with the author of the *Gospel of Judas,* the debate might sound something like this:

Irenaeus: You heretics reject the God and creator of the world who sent Jesus to die for our sins. And contrary to the clear evidence of Scripture, you deny the goodness of the Creator and his creation. You may practice a strict ethics, but only as evidence that you hate the flesh. By denying that Jesus had a physical body and that believers will rise from the dead even as Jesus did, you undermine salvation and make meaningless the church's eucharist of bread and wine (as Jesus's body and blood). You think that you are saved because of your spiritual nature and heavenly origin, so you don't need faith in Christ. Instead you claim to have special knowledge revealed to you alone. This elitist attitude is not only arrogant, it's completely in error and you will be condemned forever.[5]

The *Gospel of Judas's* author: Irenaeus, you and Christians like you have grossly mistaken the world Creator — whom Scripture itself clearly shows to be jealous, violent, and vengeful — for the true God and father of the Savior Jesus. It is you who deny the divine goodness of the true

35

God and Creator of all, who is purely goodness, light, and truth, by falsely attributing to God all maner of evil and all the ills of the world: suffering, death, unjust rule, violence, lust for the blood of sacrifice, and their like. By insisting that the physical body is your true nature, you have forgotten that the flesh is manifestly perishable, while God is imperishable. While the body can indeed worship God in righteousness, it is not immortal even though it has been stamped with the divine image of the heavenly Adam and Eve. You are like those who condemn everyone who disagrees with you to eternal punishment, arrogantly believing that you alone possess the truth. It is you who will perish forever.

Irenaeus is trying to win this argument by claiming his version of Christianity comes directly from Jesus's most trusted disciples — but the *Gospel of Judas* is making the same claim, in an extreme form: that only Judas truly understood Jesus's teaching, because Jesus revealed to him alone the true "mysteries of the kingdom."

Arguments like these were going on at a time when the church had no defined creed, no canon of authoritative texts, and no hierarchical leadership that could settle disagreements. Indeed, it was Irenaeus and his fellow bishops who decided that the marks of the "true Church" were to be creed, clergy, and canon. Irenaeus was among the first to insist that all true Christians must confess the same things,[6] joining together to say a common creed that states what all believe. He also divided the churches between bishops and priests, and "the laity" (the Greek term means "the people"), arguing that the latter must "obey the priests that are in the church,"[7] and receive baptism and eucharist only at the hands of bishops and priests he called "orthodox." He warned that dissenters, even if they were priests, placed themselves in mortal danger, since "outside the church there is no salvation." Finally, Irenaeus planted the seeds of what would become the Christian New Testament by arguing that "orthodox" believers must read during worship only books that he and other bishops approved; others, which he called "secret, illegitimate" books,[8] were to be rejected like poison — for heresy, he admonished, can draw people away from the truth. Historians have noted, too, that the teachings Irenaeus labeled as "orthodox" tend to be those that helped him and other bishops consolidate scattered groups of Jesus's followers into what he and certain other bishops envisioned as a single, united organization they called "the catholic ('universal') church." The diverse range of Christian teachings that they denounced as "heresy" could be antithetical to the consolidation of the church under the bishops' authority. Such writings as the *Gospel of Thomas* and the *Gospel of Mary,* for example, encourage believers to seek God within themselves, with no mention of churches, much less of clergy. Some writings discovered among such discarded "heretical" texts, like the *Apocalypse of Peter,* directly challenge "those who name themselves bishops . . . as if they have received their authority from God. . . . Those people are dry canals!"[9] Not surprisingly, leaders concerned about establishing and strengthening developing institutional structures dismissed such charges as the rants of "heretics" — exactly as Irenaeus condemned the *Gospel of Judas* as a piece of fiction intended merely to confuse people.

Certainly, Irenaeus would have felt his concerns validated by a work like the *Gospel of Judas.* He does not tell us whether he actually read the *Gospel of Judas* or whether he had only heard of it from others. In either case, what he knew about it outraged him. What upset him most is what still startles us: the perspective on Judas, who here appears as Jesus's most trusted — and trustworthy — disciple. According to this gospel, when Jesus challenges his disciples to stand up to him, Judas alone shows the courage to do so:

> And they all said, "We are strong!" But their spirits did not have the courage to stand up to face him — except Judas [Is]cariot. He was able to stand up to face him, even though he was not able to look him in the eyes, bu[t] turned his face aside.
> Judas said to him, "I know who you are and which place you came from." (*Judas* 2:18–22).

At this point, Jesus chooses Judas, and tells him, "Separate from them. I will tell you the mysteries of the kingdom. It is possible for you to reach that place, but you will suffer much grief" (*Judas* 2:25–28). Judas, distressed and agitated, later tells Jesus about a potent dream in which, he says, "I saw myself in a vision. The twelve disciples were stoning me; they were persecuting [me severe]ly" (*Judas* 9:6–8). Since Judas's dream alerts him to the hatred and vilification that his fellow disciples will later heap upon him, Jesus reassures him, telling him that participating in this divine mystery is his destiny, one that surpasses that of all other disciples:

> "As for you, you will surpass them all. For you will sacrifice the human being who bears me. . . . Behold, everything has been told to you. Lift up your eyes and see the cloud and the light which is in it and the stars which surround it. And the star that leads the way, that is your star" (*Judas* 15:3–4, 14–16).

Equally upsetting, however, is that the *Gospel of Judas* pictures the other disciples — "the twelve," whom Irenaeus revered as the founders of the present succession of bishops — as fools who worshipped false gods and committed all kinds of sins, including murder.

These kinds of arguments make it clear that various Christians in the second century were calling upon certain apostles to legitimize their own interpretations of Christianity. But that only leaves open the question of what actually happened in the events leading up to Jesus's arrest. Do the early Christian gospels offer solid historical evidence? What, if anything, does the *Gospel of Judas* tell us that is new? Answering these questions requires us to look again at the four gospels long familiar from the New Testament to see what they tell us and how they agree — and disagree — with one another, for their authors, too, are struggling to understand the role of Judas, and each tells the story differently. After that, we can see how this new gospel relates to what may actually have happened.

In all the gospels, one historical event stands out as virtually certain: that Jesus of Nazareth was crucified around 33 C.E., during the reign of Emperor Tiberius, when Pontius Pilate was chief Roman officer in Judea. On this point all our sources agree — even first- and second-century writers hostile to Jesus. Josephus, the Jewish governor of Galilee (C. 50 C.E.) who wrote the famous history *The Jewish War,* mentions Jesus as a notorious troublemaker.[10] Tacitus, the Roman senator and orator who detests Christians, explains to his readers who they are, and why they are so disruptive, in these words:

Christus, from whom the name originated, suffered the extreme penalty during the reign of Tiberius, under one of our procurators, Pontius Pilate, and a deadly superstition, thus checked for the moment, again broke out not only in Judea, the first source of the evil, but also in the City (Rome) where everything hideous and shameful from every part of the world meets and becomes popular.[11]

That Jesus was crucified is acknowledged not only by every one of the four New Testament gospels and the letters of Paul but also by many gospels *outside* the New Testament, including the *Gospel of Truth,* the *Gospel of Philip,* the *Secret Book of James,* the *Apocalypse of Peter,* and the *Letter of Peter to Philip,* to mention only a few. But when these followers try to say what Jesus's execution could mean, agreement ends. For those who left the movement it seemed that the crucifixion proved that Jesus was not God's chosen one, or at least that God had abandoned him. Paul admits that when he preached among Jews, the terrible fact that Jesus had been crucified presented a nearly insurmountable obstacle to any who heard him; among Gentiles, his claims about an executed criminal sounded ridiculous (*I Corinthians* 1:17–24). Outsiders confirm this: The philosopher Celsus says that many people despised Christians because, in his words, "they worship a crucified sophist."[12] Yet for Paul, the meaning was clear: "Christ died for our sins in accordance with the scriptures" (*I Corinthians* 15:3).

Others devoted to Jesus, like the author of the *Gospel of Mark,* expressed concerns about what Jesus's crucifixion might mean. But unlike Paul, the *Gospel of Mark* addressed the problem by constructing a detailed story about Jesus's arrest and execution. What could it mean to proclaim that Jesus not only *was* but still *is* God's anointed king when the gospel admits that he fell, helpless, into Roman hands to be tortured and killed, abandoned by everyone, and even, as Jesus himself cried out as he died, abandoned by God (*Mark* 15:34)? How could the story the author tells possibly be what his opening words led the hearer to expect — "the *good news* of Jesus Christ, the Son of God" (*Mark* 1:1)? We might expect the author of the *Gospel of Mark* to emphasize that Jesus rose from the dead, but in his account the resurrection remains a future event, at which the narrative only hints.[13] What the *Gospel of Mark* offers here is much more than simple narrative history: The author calls it "gospel" — preaching — set forth in the form of interpretive narrative in order to convey spiritual meaning.

This earliest gospel proved enormously influential, since the authors of the *Gospels of Matthew* and *Luke,* writing about ten to thirty years after the *Gospel of Mark* was written, both copied much of what its author wrote, sometimes nearly word for word, into their own, longer, gospel narratives. Each of them based his own gospel on the *Gospel of Mark*'s story line and amplified what he found in the *Gospel of Mark* by adding more material, in the process giving his own emphasis and interpretation of the story.

When they wrote about Jesus's arrest, for example, each one, including the author of the *Gospel of Mark,* had to explain how Jesus's enemies succeeded in capturing him. What, then, do they say about Judas? The evidence suggests that Jesus's followers knew that someone had betrayed him, a person the *Gospel of Mark* names as Judas Iscariot. Baffled and troubled by this betrayer, they pondered, discussed, and argued about what he did and why. The author of *Mark's Gospel,* who wrote the earliest version we have of the story, apparently includes Judas among the disciples who it says heard Peter blurt out to Jesus, "You are the

Messiah" (*Mark* 8:29). But the *Gospel of Mark* says that immediately afterward, Jesus confided to them that he expected to suffer terribly and be killed by his enemies. When Peter, shocked and troubled, expressed horror, Jesus's response was unexpectedly harsh: "Get behind me, Satan!" indicating that he could not — would not — evade what he insisted must happen, a necessary course of events, divinely ordained. To make this clear, the author of the *Gospel of Mark* has Jesus ask two of his followers to help stage a messianic demonstration of a peasant king riding a donkey into Jerusalem, in fulfillment of an oracle of the prophet Zechariah:

Rejoice greatly, O daughter Zion! Shout aloud, O daughter Jerusalem! Lo, your king comes to you; triumphant and victorious is he, humble, and riding on a donkey, on a colt, the foal of a donkey (*Zechariah* 9:9).

Then, before Jesus shared the Passover meal with his disciples, right after he repeated his prediction that he would die, the author of the *Gospel of Mark* says that "Judas Iscariot, who was one of the twelve, went to the chief priests in order to betray him to them" (*Mark* 14:10). Intriguingly, the author refrains from suggesting a motive. Yet he does speculate that the chief priests gladly seized on the opportunity Judas offered them, hoping to find Jesus and his followers alone at night, apart from the crowds that often surrounded him, in order to kill him. The author of the *Gospel of Mark* says that they offered to pay Judas, apparently to add incentive: "When they heard it, they were greatly pleased, and promised to give him money" (*Mark* 14:11).

The author of *Mark's Gospel* apparently knows that some people were saying what the *Gospel of Judas* says explicitly — that Judas is doing precisely what must be done to further God's plan, perhaps in obedience to an order given him by Jesus. But the author of the *Gospel of Mark* counters that suggestion in his own account, by having Jesus solemnly declare that "the Son of Man goes as it is written of him, but woe to that one by whom the Son of Man is betrayed! It would have been better for that one not to have been born" (*Mark* 14:21). Finally, the *Gospel of Mark* says that when Judas arrived in Gethsemane with a crowd of armed men, he already

. . . had given them a sign, saying, "The

one I will kiss is the man; arrest him and lead him away under guard." So when he came, he went up to (Jesus) at once and said, "Rabbi!" and kissed him. Then they laid hands on him and arrested him (*Mark* 14:44–46).

The author of the *Gospel of Matthew* must have been powerfully impressed with the *Gospel of Mark,* since he took it up, changing only a few details, expanded it with other sayings attributed to Jesus, and added some stories not known elsewhere, to make a new version. When we look at the additions and changes he made, we can see that the authority that mattered above all to the writer we call Matthew was that of his Scriptures, namely, the Hebrew Bible. It was to those Jewish Scriptures that he turned when perplexed and troubled; so naturally he turned to them to make some sense out of Judas's betrayal. Rereading books such as *Genesis,* the *Psalms,* and the prophets' writings while pondering the story of Judas, the author of the *Gospel of Matthew* found there passages and allusions which suggested to him that the betrayal itself was part of God's plan. Keeping these passages in mind, he rewrote the *Gospel of Mark's* story elaborating the bare fact of the betrayal and even inverting scenes so that certain details correlated more precisely with those prophecies, as we shall see. The author of the *Gospel of Matthew* no doubt found consolation in believing that the prophecies placed these terrible events into the context of the divine plan, which he said God had revealed through the Holy Spirit.

The most striking change the *Gospel of Matthew* made was to suggest a motive. Instead of simply following the author of the *Gospel of Mark,* who, as we noted, says that the chief priests offered Judas money as an added incentive only after he had offered to betray Jesus, the *Gospel of Matthew's* author turns the story around. In order to show that what motivated Judas was greed, he says Judas was the one who initiated negotiations with the chief priests by demanding money: "Then one of the twelve, who was called Judas Iscariot, went to the chief priests and said, 'What will you give me if I betray him to you?' They paid him thirty pieces of silver" (*Matthew* 26:14–15). Mentioning this specific amount, the author of the *Gospel of Matthew* knew, would resonate with those familiar with the Scriptures, especially with famous passages from the prophet Zechariah. The *Gospel of Matthew* actually has Jesus himself compare his own impending fate to that of the prophets, and above all, Zechariah, who was killed in the temple, "murdered between the sanctuary and the altar" *(Matthew* 23:34–35). "Thirty pieces of silver" was the contemptible price at which rulers of Israel valued Zechariah (*Zechariah* 11:12–13), exactly the same amount, the author of the *Gospel of Matthew* wants to show, that the Jerusalem leaders paid for Jesus, and with the same feelings of contempt. The *Gospel of Matthew* also applies to Jesus the prophet Isaiah's vision of Israel as God's suffering slave (*Isaiah* 53:3–12; *Matthew* 8:17), and thus, no doubt, appreciated the irony of having thirty pieces of silver, the biblical price for a slave (*Exodus* 21:32), paid not only for Zechariah but as the price for Jesus's life as well. When Zechariah goes on to lament his own fate, seeing himself as "a shepherd of the flock doomed to slaughter" (*Zechariah* 11:4), the author of the *Gospel of Matthew* takes this, too, as prefiguring what happened to Jesus.

Finally, while the *Gospel of Mark* had said nothing of what happened to Judas later, the author of the *Gospel of Matthew,* having pictured Judas corrupted by greed and betraying Jesus for money, takes another cue from Zechariah to tell "the moral of the story." Of all the New Testament gospels, the famous account of Judas's remorse, despair, and suicide is found only in the *Gospel of Matthew's* version.[14] Thus, having noted what Zechariah says he did with the money ("I took the thirty shekels of silver and threw them into the treasury in the house of the Lord"), the author of the *Gospel of Matthew* writes that Judas tried to do the same:

> When Judas, his betrayer, saw that Jesus was condemned, he repented and brought back the thirty pieces of silver to the chief priests and the elders. He said, "I have sinned by betraying innocent blood." But they said, "What is that to us? See to it yourself." Throwing down the pieces of silver in the temple, he departed; and he went and hanged himself (*Matthew* 27:3–5).

But the *Gospel of Matthew* goes on to say that Judas could not even throw the money back into the Temple treasury, as Zechariah had, since his money was polluted by blood guilt:

> (T)he chief priests, taking the pieces of silver, said, "It is not lawful to put them

into the treasury, since they are blood money." After conferring together, they used them to buy the potter's field as a place to bury foreigners. For this reason that field has been called the Field of Blood to this day (*Matthew* 27:6–18).[15]

The *Gospel of Matthew* declares that these events "fulfilled what had been spoken by the prophet Jeremiah," as he concludes the story with an episode suggested by *Zechariah* 11:12–13 amplified by Jeremiah's prophetic vision of God judging the wicked as a potter deciding to break his defective vessels (*Jeremiah* 18:1–3; 19:1–13, conflated with the story of the potter's field).

The author of the *Gospel of Luke* also knows the *Gospel of Mark,* and he incorporates much of its sixteen chapters into his own writing. He not only changes details — often crucial ones — but also adds a diverse collection of anecdotes about Jesus and teachings attributed to him. At the same time, he, too, interpreted and embellished the traditions he knew from his deep familiarity with the Hebrew Bible. Thus he told the story of John the Baptist's birth, for example, to recall the birth of Isaac to the aged Abraham and Sarah (*Luke* 1:5–25), for John's parents too, he said, were not only childless but past their childbearing years (*Luke* 1:7). Luke next tells the story of Mary's miraculous conception to recall the story of Samuel's birth to the childless Hannah, answering her prayers (*Luke* 1:26–56). Casting the glow of biblical precedent over the story helped Christians dispel embarrassing rumors that swirled around Jesus's questionable birth. Both gospel authors knew, of course, that hostile critics were charging that Jesus was born fatherless, and so illegitimate; thus both went to great lengths to show instead that his birth was a miracle.[16]

But when the gospel writers came to tell the whole story of Jesus's betrayal, arrest, and death, they had to deal with a far greater embarrassment. For how could anyone claim that a man shamefully tortured and crucified by the Romans not only *was* but still *is* the messiah, as the *Gospel of Luke* proclaims? And to admit, as the *Gospel of Luke* does, that one of Jesus's intimate disciples had led armed men to the hill where they found him that night and had tried to kiss him to identify him (*Luke* 22:47–48), could only compound their distress. Thus the author of *Luke,* too, sought for scriptural references to place this shocking betrayal into the context of what prophets had predicted, to show that nothing that happened was out of God's control but that, on the contrary, every detail formed part of God's plan.

The author of the *Gospel of Luke,* too, wondered why Judas went to Jesus's enemies and offered to betray him. If he even knew the *Gospel of Matthew's* version, apparently he thought that wanting money was not a strong enough motive to account for such a drastic act; thus he says nothing to indicate Judas was greedy. Instead, he adds three words to the account in the *Gospel of Mark* to include what some people must have been saying: that the Evil One, who had stalked Jesus since he began his public preaching (*Luke* 4:1–13), had now returned to catch his prey. For when Judas left the others that fatal night, the *Gospel of Luke* says, "Satan entered into Judas Iscariot, who was one of the twelve" (*Luke* 22:3). At that moment, this disciple went to initiate the conspiracy. Thus the author of the *Gospel of Luke* shows that the supernatural power of evil accomplished what human force could neither effect nor prevent.

As the *Gospel of Mark* tells it, when Judas kissed Jesus, he greeted him as "Rabbi!" But the accounts in *Luke* and *Matthew* both amplify this dramatic moment by adding dialogue. According to *Matthew's Gospel,* Judas said, "Greetings, Rabbi!" and Jesus replied (in what tone, we are left to imagine), "Friend, do what you are here to do" (*Matthew* 26:50). According to the *Gospel of Luke,* however, Jesus averted the kiss and instead directly challenged Judas:

> While (Jesus) was still speaking, suddenly a crowd came, and the one called Judas, one of the twelve, was leading them. He approached Jesus to kiss him; but Jesus said to him, "Judas, is it with a kiss that you are betraying the Son of Man?" (*Luke* 22:47–48).

Another embarrassing part of the story was the ease with which Jesus was captured while his disciples fled. Hadn't any of his followers fought to defend him? If not, why not? There is evidence in the various gospels that these questions, too, troubled the writers. The *Gospel of Mark* tells us that "one of those who stood near drew his sword and struck the slave of the high priest, cutting off his ear" (*Mark* 14:47). But at that point, the *Gospel of Mark* says, Jesus, seeing these events as his destiny, declared, "(L)et the Scriptures be fulfilled." Only at that moment does the *Gospel of Mark* say that "all of them deserted him and fled" (*Mark* 14:49–50) — a point so embarrassing that the author of the *Gospel of Luke* omits it. The *Gospel of Matthew*, however, again finds help in the oracles of *Zechariah*. For before this happens, he has Jesus predict that the disciples would abandon him, and he invokes Zechariah's words in 13:7 as prophesying this:

> Then Jesus said to them, "You will all become deserters because of me this night; for it is written, 'I will strike the shepherd, and the sheep of the flock will be scattered' " (*Matthew* 26:31).

At this point in the narrative, the *Gospel of Matthew* follows the *Gospel of Mark*'s account of how all the disciples fled. But the author adds to this that Jesus himself stopped the disciple who attacked the slave, rebuked him for using violence, and declared that he could invoke supernatural armies to protect him but had resolved not to do so:

> "Put your sword back into its place; for all who take the sword will perish by the sword. Do you think that I cannot appeal to my Father, and he will at once send me

more than twelve legions of angels? But how then would the scriptures be fulfilled, which say it must happen this way?" (*Matthew* 26:52–54)

The *Gospel of Luke* takes the story further, and adds a miracle. As the author tells it, after Jesus's disciple cut off the right ear of the high priest's slave, "Jesus said, 'No more of this!' And he touched his ear and healed him" (*Luke* 22:51).

Thus each of the gospel writers boldly confronts what Paul calls the "scandal" of Jesus's shameful death by insisting not only that Jesus had to die, as the *Gospel of Mark* put it (*Mark* 9:31), but that he did so knowing and accepting that his death was essential to God's plan of salvation.

We can see, too, that each version pictures Jesus increasingly in control of what happens. The vulnerable Jesus becomes more powerful from gospel to gospel, from earlier accounts to the later ones — that is, from the *Gospel of Mark* to *Matthew* and *Luke,* and, as we will see, to the *Gospel of John.* We can see the same pattern at work when we trace how each writer in turn describes the last supper. According to the *Gospel of Mark,* on his last night, Jesus had told his disciples that "one of you will betray me"

(*Mark* 14:18). The author noted a passage in the *Psalms* which he read as prophesying what Judas did ("Even my bosom friend in whom I trusted, who ate of my bread, has lifted the heel against me" [*Psalms* 41:9]). Keeping this in mind, the author of the *Gospel of Mark* wrote the famous episode of the last supper, in which Jesus reveals who will betray him by identifying him as one "who is dipping his bread into the bowl with me" (*Mark* 14:20).[17] Neither *Mark*'s nor *Luke*'s *Gospel* says that Jesus actually identified *any* single disciple as his betrayer, either by gesture or by name, and again the *Gospel of Luke* says only his hand was on the table (see *Luke* 22:21). It is only the *Gospel of John*'s more dramatic version that pictures Jesus positively identifying the guilty culprit. As the author of the *Gospel of John* tells it, when the disciple closest to Jesus — the one he calls "the one whom Jesus loved" — asks Jesus "who is it?" (*John* 13:25) Jesus gives a specific and definitive answer. Here, perhaps not surprisingly, Jesus's answer fits the prophecy in detail: " 'It is the one to whom I give this piece of bread, when I have dipped it in the dish.' So when he had dipped the piece of bread, he gave it to Judas son of Simon Iscariot" (*John* 13:26).

In this episode, the author of the *Gospel*

of John pictures Jesus in charge of every act in the drama — just as he does throughout the whole passion story. Even before Jesus identifies Judas, he has already told his disciples that "the hour had come" for him "to depart from this world and go to the Father" (*John* 13:1). Only after showing that Jesus anticipated and accepted his impending death does the *Gospel of John,* like the *Gospel of Luke,* say that the power of evil had overtaken Judas: "The devil had already put it into the heart of Judas son of Simon Iscariot to betray him" (*John* 13:2). But to show that Jesus is in control even of Satan's entry into Judas, John declares that only "after (Judas) received (from Jesus) the piece of bread, Satan entered into him" (*John* 13:27). And at that moment, Jesus gave Judas an order: "Do quickly what you are going to do" (*John* 13:27). The *Gospel of John* says that no one else at the table knew what this meant, although some thought that Jesus's command had to do with Judas's responsibilities for managing the group's funds. Shortly before, the *Gospel of John* had identified Judas as a thieving, greedy man who criticized others to display his own piety (*John* 12:4–6). As *John*'s author tells it, Jesus not only refused to allow Judas to kiss him, but Jesus himself took the initiative — not once, but twice — to identify *himself* to the men who came to arrest him. So, when Judas arrived, leading "a detachment of soldiers, together with police" who brought torches, lanterns, and weapons,

> (t)hen Jesus, knowing all that was going to happen, came forward and asked them, "Whom are you looking for?" They answered, "Jesus of Nazareth." Jesus replied, "I am he." Judas, who betrayed him, was standing with them. When Jesus said to them, "I am he," they stepped back and fell to the ground. Again he asked them, "Whom are you looking for?" And they said, "Jesus of Nazareth." Jesus answered, "I told you that I am he. So if you are looking for me, let these men go" (*John* 18:4–8).

As the soldiers retreat and fall on the ground, helpless before him, it becomes clear that here it is Jesus who gives the orders — even telling the soldiers whom to arrest and whom to let go.

When we look at the *Gospel of Judas,* then, we can see that all this author does is to take one step further this tendency to show Jesus in control. Just as the *Gospel of*

Mark says that Jesus instructed specific disciples to set up the Passover meal and his entry into Jerusalem, and just as the *Gospel of John* says that Jesus himself told Judas to go out and "do what you have to do," so too the *Gospel of Judas* says that Jesus told Judas to hand him over, so that what had to happen could happen. But the *Gospel of Judas* ends the story there. There is no story of arrest, no torture, no crucifixion, no resurrection. As a result, the *Gospel of Judas* succeeds in shifting the focus from Jesus's death to what he reveals to Judas before he dies — the mysteries of the kingdom.

But where in all this is the history? What really happened? Through the centuries Christians have taken authors at their word not only that all these events happened as the New Testament gospel writers say but that they were prophesied hundreds of years before they happened, thus reassuring believers that every detail occurred as it was meant to. Today, New Testament scholars differ in judgment about what and how much in the gospel stories is based on actual history. By comparing the accounts we can see that the gospel writers elaborated on stories of Jesus's death in order to express the theological points they wanted to emphasize — and to address the basic problem that God's messiah had been put to a horrible death as a criminal at the hands of the occupying Roman government. How much did they invent? Is it possible that those events, which are so clearly inspired by the prophetic writings, were actually written *from* them, with no historical basis at all? The New Testament scholar John Dominic Crossan puts the question this way: Are the details of the crucifixion accounts "history prophesied" or are they "prophecy historicized"?[18]

There clearly are cases where the gospel writers invented episodes from passages of prophetic oracles. Compare, for example, how the authors of the *Gospels of Mark* and *Matthew* narrate Jesus's "triumphal entry" on the day that Christians call Palm Sunday. We noted earlier how the author of *Mark's Gospel* tells the story: that Jesus rode into Jerusalem on a donkey, acclaimed by his followers as King of Israel. The author of the *Gospel of Matthew* noted, of course, that the author of the *Gospel of Mark* had Zechariah's prophecy in mind when he wrote this scene, and he wrote several additional lines into the story. When the author of *Matthew* retells the story, he actually places directly before it his own paraphrase of

Zechariah's oracle in 9:9: "Tell the daughter of Zion, Look, your king is coming to you, humble, and mounted on a donkey, and on a colt, the foal of a donkey" (*Matthew* 21:5). But careful as the author was to track Zechariah's oracle as he wrote, he seems not to have noticed that the last phrase of this prophecy involves the well-known literary device of poetic repetition. It appears that the author of the *Gospel of Matthew* was so intent on making the scene correspond to prophecy as closely as possible that he changed the *Gospel of Mark*'s narrative to say that Jesus ordered his disciples to bring him both a donkey *and* a colt. The result is that the *Gospel of Matthew* gives a rather ridiculous picture of Jesus riding into Jerusalem straddling two animals at once: "The disciples went and did as Jesus had directed them; they brought the donkey and the colt, and put their cloaks on them, and he sat on them" (*Matthew* 21:6–7).

How far does this invention go? Did the authors of the *Gospels of Matthew* and *Mark* invent the story of Judas's betrayal as well? Some scholars argue that the gospel writers took *Isaiah*'s vision of God's suffering slave as a prophecy that Jesus would be betrayed, that is, "handed over for our sins," as one version of the Greek translation suggests.[19]

When Jesus's followers asked who could possibly have betrayed him, some suggest that the authors of the *Gospels of Mark* and *Matthew* thought they had found an answer in *Psalm* 41:9: "My bosom friend in whom I trusted, who ate of my bread, has lifted the heel against me." When the disciples were at supper with Jesus the night before he died, they asked him the same question — who would betray him? The *Gospels of Mark* and *Matthew* tell us that his answer echoed the words of David's prophecy:

> . . . while they were eating, (Jesus) said, "Truly I tell you, one of you will betray me." And they became greatly distressed and began to say to him one after another, "Surely not I, Lord?" He answered, "The one who has dipped his hand in the bowl with me will betray me" (*Matthew* 26:20–23).

Scholars who see this story as "prophecy historicized" have argued that the gospel writers selected passages like these and pieced them together to come up with the story of Judas. Some conclude, then, that the account of Judas's betrayal has no historical basis whatsoever.[20]

While this is not impossible, it leaves the

question of why Jesus's followers would have made it up. For to admit that one of Jesus's closest followers actually had turned upon him and betrayed him was an enormous disgrace. If it was not true, would Jesus's followers have risked bringing such shame upon the movement? And if someone outside the group had invented a character like this, wouldn't Jesus's followers have been likely to denounce it as a slanderous lie? Since the story was widely known and not challenged, it is likely that someone in the movement did betray Jesus.[21] For as we have seen, instead of denying this embarrassing fact, the New Testament gospel writers all attempted only to mitigate its impact — first, by claiming that Jesus knew and accepted what would happen; second, by placing this event, too, in the context of prophecies, to show that nothing, however horrible, happens apart from God's divine plan.

Even when dealing with events they knew had happened, then, the gospels writers searched through the Jewish Scriptures for prophecies that seemed to fit them, just as King David's lament over a friend's betrayal in *Psalm* 41 could be read as prophesying Judas betraying Jesus. Often we can see that the historicity of events matters less to the gospel authors than the moral lesson they want to convey — in the case of Judas's suicide, for example, that evil brings ruin.

Each gospel, then, retells Jesus's death as a way to emphasize the theological points the author wants to make: For the *Gospel of Mark,* that it was necessary for God's messiah to suffer and die in order to usher in the kingdom of God and the final end of all things. The *Gospel of Matthew* argues that everything that happened was part of God's plan, even when Judas acted out of that most human of faults — greed. For the *Gospel of Luke,* that Jesus is depicted as utterly in control, even of Satan himself, who enters Judas in order to bring God's plan to completion. The *Gospel of John* goes furthest, portraying Jesus directing all the events, even his own betrayal.[22] The *Gospel of Judas* is, then, only one more retelling of a much-told tale, but it gives this story a radical new twist, one that turns the tables on "the twelve."

CHAPTER TWO:
JUDAS AND THE TWELVE

Once we see that all the New Testament gospels treat Judas's betrayal as God's will, it seems less strange to think that Judas might have been seen as following Jesus's instructions in handing him over, as the *Gospel of Judas* says. More surprising is the way the *Gospel of Judas* turns upside down what we know about the other disciples — or what we thought we knew. This gospel does more than champion the disciple that all the rest regard as the villain; it also sharply condemns "the twelve." For when they come to Jesus, disturbed by a dream they had of priests at the altar who are sacrificing their own wives and children and committing all kinds of sins and injustices — and doing so in Jesus's name — his reply shocks and angers them: "*You* are the ones you saw receiving offerings at the altar. . . . And the domestic animals you saw being brought for sacrifice are the multitude you are leading astray upon that al[t]ar" (*Judas* 5:1; 4). Here the very disciples revered by many Christians as leaders and founders of the movement appear as if it is they — not Judas — who are betraying Jesus.

Radically as this reverses the traditional gospel story, when we compare this newly discovered gospel with the New Testament, we can see that the author of the *Gospel of Judas* is merely doing what other Christians did — for not only does virtually every gospel elevate one or more disciples over all the rest, they also frequently relate stories about the disciples in conflict with one another. These stories are important to historians because they let us see early Christians vying with one another for power, and they tell us a lot about what issues the earliest believers were struggling over.

The *Gospel of Mark,* for example, pictures Peter as the designated leader of the group after Jesus's death, claiming that Peter is the first to recognize who Jesus is — God's messiah — even though Peter later misunderstands and even denies that he knows Jesus (*Mark* 8:27–33; 14:53–72). The *Gospel of Matthew* emphatically affirms Peter's primacy and even adds a claim — unique to his gospel — that Jesus himself declared that

God chose Peter to reveal who Jesus is, and to be the foundation stone for the future church:

> Jesus answered (Peter), "Blessed are you, Simon, son of Jonah! For flesh and blood has not revealed this to you, but my Father in heaven. And I tell you, you are Peter (*petros*), and on this rock (*petra*) I will build my church, and the gates of Hades will not prevail against it. I will give you the keys of the kingdom of heaven, and whatever you bind on earth will be bound in heaven, and whatever you loose on earth will be loosed in heaven" (*Matthew* 16:17–19).

From this ringing endorsement of Peter that the author of *Matthew's Gospel* puts in the mouth of Jesus, Christians in later generations developed the picture of Peter as the gatekeeper of heaven — the one who decides who enters the "pearly gates" in heaven and also wields divine authority on earth.

The author of the two-volume work the *Gospel of Luke* and the *Acts of the Apostles* tells a somewhat different story: that Jesus declares that all of "the twelve" will reign with him as his council in the coming kingdom, even though he also tells several stories to show that among "the twelve," Peter has priority and speaks for all the apostles as their undisputed leader (*Luke* 22:29–32; 24:34; *Acts* 1:15, 2:14).

Yet when we look at other early writings — both within the New Testament and outside of it — we can see that other Christians disputed attempts to elevate Peter, questioning his judgment and character; some advocated the leadership of others instead. The *Gospel of John,* for example, gives a different picture of Jesus's disciples. The author of the *Gospel of John* acknowledges that Peter is prominent among the disciples but consistently pictures him as only *second* to the one the author regards as the greatest among the disciples — the one he simply calls "the disciple whom Jesus loved" (*John* 13:23). This gospel acknowledges Peter as a legitimate leader but places the beloved disciple above him as a greater leader. As the *Gospel of John* tells it, the "one whom Jesus loved" raced Peter to the tomb and got there first, and although he wasn't the first to go in, he — not Peter — was the first to believe that Jesus was risen from the dead. Even more, the *Gospel of John* goes on to show that Mary Magdalene, not Peter, was the first to see and speak with the risen Jesus, and was commissioned by him to announce the resurrection to the other disciples (*John* 20:1–4, 8, 11–18). Both "the beloved disciple" and Mary thus here outrank Peter as primary witnesses to the resurrection.

The *Gospel of Thomas,* like the *Gospel of John,* includes Peter among the disciples' leaders but suggests that it was Thomas who had received a deeper understanding of Jesus's gospel. Yet according to the *Gospel of Thomas,* when Jesus's disciples asked him, "Who will be our leader after you are gone?" Jesus said to them, "Go to James the Just" — referring, apparently, to Jesus's brother (cf. *Mark* 6:3), whom many regarded as Jesus's rightful successor. According to tradition, James headed one of the earliest groups of Jesus's followers, based in Jerusalem, until around 62 C.E., when he was purportedly thrown down from a parapet and clubbed to death.[1] To this day, the Church of St. James in Jerusalem, where the bishop of the Armenian Orthodox Church presides, celebrates James, not Peter, as Jesus's primary apostle.

The *Gospel of Thomas* also relates a dispute between Peter and Mary of Magdala, in which Peter says to Jesus, "Tell

Mary to leave us, for women are not worthy of (spiritual) life." But instead of dismissing Mary, as Peter insists, Jesus rebukes Peter, and declares, "I will make Mary a living spirit,"[2] so that she — or any woman — may become as capable of spiritual life as any man. A whole cluster of early writings, above all the *Gospel of Mary*, tell of arguments that broke out between Peter and Mary.[3] The *Gospel of Mary* pictures her taking a leading role among the disciples when she found the others terrified to preach the gospel after Jesus's death, fearing that they, like their leader, would be arrested and killed. At this point, Mary stands up to speak and encourages them, "turning their heart toward the Good" (*Mary* 5:9).[4] Then Peter, acknowledging that "the Savior loved you more than other women," asks Mary to "tell us those words of the Savior which you know, but which we haven't heard" (*Mary* 6:2). But when Mary agrees and tells Peter that she will now share with him what Jesus had kept secret from the other disciples, Peter, jealous, asks, "Did he, then, speak with a woman in private without our knowing about it? Are we to turn around and listen to her? Did he choose her over us?" (*Mary* 10:3–4). Distressed at his rage, Mary replies, "My brother Peter, what are you imagining?

71

Do you think that I have thought up these things by myself in my heart or that I am telling lies about the Savior?" (*Mary* 10:5–6). Levi breaks in at this point to mediate the dispute:

> "Peter, you are always ready to give way to your perpetual inclination to anger. And even now you are doing exactly that by questioning the woman as though you're her adversary. If the Savior considered her to be worthy, who are you to disregard her? Assuredly the Savior's knowledge of her is completely reliable. That is why he loved her more than us" (*Mary* 10:7–10).

By elevating one or more disciples over the others, each of these stories makes a claim about who speaks for Jesus now that he is gone. Each attempts to answer the questions: Who has his power now? Who is to replace him? Who has the strongest connection with Jesus, and whose vision can be trusted? The practical effect of these stories — and, no doubt, one of their purposes — has been to limit the circle of authorized people to a small, specifically named group of disciples. As the *Acts of the Apostles* tells it, those to whom Jesus directly conveyed his authority, like "the twelve," later "laid their hands on them" to transmit the divine power they had received onto others as well (*Acts* 6:6). Today many Christian churches ritualize that process in the rite called "ordination," in which a bishop or other minister "places hands upon" a person to convey divine authority — a process practiced in various ways from the first century down to the present in churches throughout the world, and one which often is used for a similar purpose: to try to settle disputes over power and precedence by authorizing a few or excluding other voices from the conversation.

Yet the New Testament gospels and letters go further than elevating some disciples over the rest. They also show us what issues divided believers during those formative years. The dispute between Peter and Mary in the *Gospel of Mary,* for example, suggests that one question proved explosively controversial: Can a woman be a leader among the disciples — or can she even be a disciple at all? Even today, Christians often invoke these gospels, along with other canonical texts like *I Timothy,* to "prove" that women cannot hold positions of authority within Christian churches, but in fact the issue was hotly debated, as stories depicting controversies between Mary and Peter show.[5]

When Christians in later generations told stories of rivalry between disciples, then, and chose which stories to tell and which to leave out, often they were taking sides in disputes between different groups. Stories of conflict between disciples often dramatized tensions over specific — and practical — issues; most often, however, such conflicts did not split groups apart. Quite frequently an author tells about a dispute in order to correct some kind of error on the part of the disciples. For example, according to the *Gospel of Mark,* the two brothers James and John "came forward to (Jesus) and said to him, 'Rabbi, we want you to do for us whatever we ask of you.' " When Jesus asked what they wanted, they admitted that they wanted him to promise that he would make the two of them his chief advisers in the coming kingdom; when the other disciples heard of it, quite understandably "they began to be angry with James and John." But Jesus goes on to tell them they have misunderstood the very nature of discipleship — that prominence in the group will come not to those who seek it for themselves (*Mark* 10:35–45). Discipleship means giving up one's life — and one's power — in order to serve others.[6]

Recognizing that the New Testament

gospels contain many such stories in which Jesus's followers are portrayed as disagreeing, we can see that despite their disagreements, those on both sides of the argument usually remained within the same community. Most conflicts the gospels describe show that Christian groups, then as now, were able to accept a variety of viewpoints on controversial issues without dividing. Although later tradition often insisted that all the voices included in the New Testament collection say virtually the same thing, we can see many differences among them, and those who gathered them into the canon tolerated considerable diversity of viewpoint, so to speak, "within the family."

Diversity, then, is nothing new. On the contrary, our earliest sources show that only twenty years after Jesus's death, Paul was dismayed to find various groups of his followers affiliating themselves with different teachers. Paul scolded Christians in the Greek port city of Corinth for "jealousy and quarreling among you. . . . For when one says, 'I belong to Paul,' and another, 'I belong to Apollos,' are you not merely human?" (*I Corinthians* 3:3–4).

But in spite of this, Paul was the first, so far as we know, to open up a dispute that threatened to split the movement apart. In his *Letter to the Galatians,* Paul calls Peter a hypocrite and denounces him for refusing to eat with non–Jewish believers (2:11–21). As he tells it, when Peter came to meet Paul in Syria, he initially shared meals with Paul and his Gentile followers, which meant that Peter was temporarily ignoring the kosher diet that he ordinarily observed. But Paul says that when other followers of Jesus arrived, coming from the group led by James, Peter stopped sharing his meals with Gentiles. Indignant, Paul publicly accused Peter of being a hypocrite who acted out of fear of what other Jews would think — and failed to act according to what Paul insisted was "the truth of the gospel" (*Galatians* 2:5). Paul vehemently declared to his Gentile followers that anyone who taught "a gospel contrary to what we proclaimed to you" — even if that one was "an angel from heaven" — or, he implied, Peter himself — "let him be accursed!" And lest anyone think he was only speaking impulsively, Paul emphatically repeats the curse in writing: "As we have said before, so now I repeat: if anyone proclaims to you a gospel contrary to what you received, let that one be accursed!" (*Galatians* 1:9). For Paul, Jesus's death was the signal that God had extended the promise of salvation to all people; to continue to obey exclusionary table practices was tantamount to denying that truth of the gospel. When one leader curses another, as Paul does here, conflicts can quickly erupt into schism, as may have happened when the people who thought that converts had to be circumcised and to obey Jewish table practices broke with other Christians.

At its beginnings, the Christian movement was fragile, often wracked by strife, as the New Testament documents so clearly. But why do many people have the opposite impression — of the early church as a unified and harmonious communion of believers living together in joyful prayer and worship, holding whatever they had as common property, "of one heart and soul"? (*Acts* 4:32). And why do most Christians today think of Peter and Paul as brother apostles who shared the struggles of the early days together — not, as Paul himself describes them, as rivals engaged in bitter fighting over the meaning of Jesus's death?

This impression is no accident. Instead, it was carefully constructed by the author who wrote the *Gospel of Luke* and the *Acts of the Apostles.* For this author wanted to stop disagreement from leading to schism, so he chose to gloss over the harsh infighting between Peter and Paul and offered instead an exemplary picture in the *Acts of the Apostles* to illustrate how believers *ought* to resolve their differences.[7] *Acts* tells how a meeting of the apostles and elders was convened in Jerusalem. After discussing Paul's preaching to Gentiles — which it said had stirred up "no small dissention and debate" — James, the elder statesman of the group, stood up and proposed a compromise solution, which the whole congregation accepted and then circulated in a letter to all Gentile believers (*Acts* 15:1–35). The author of *Luke-Acts* no doubt intended his picture of the early church's harmony to nurture the spirit of unity — precisely because he recognized that what we often call the early church actually consisted of clusters of diverse and scattered groups of believers. Few leaders condemned others as harshly as Paul cursing Peter. But as we have seen, such local conflicts involved more than personal rivalries or power struggles; at the same time, they raise central issues: Who really understands the "gospel" — and how should it be practiced? Should slaves — free in Christ — be emancipated from their earthly masters? Should Gentile converts observe Jewish laws — and if so, which ones? Which leaders can be trusted?

Strife, too, marks the *Gospel of Judas.*

What are we to make of the strangest parts of the *Gospel of Judas* — the passages in which Jesus attacks "the twelve," laughs at them, dismisses their worship, tells them to stop sacrificing, and pictures them as evil priests who slaughter human beings — murdering even their own wives and children — to please their God? How can it claim that it is not Judas but "the twelve" who betray Jesus?

Are these the ravings of a mad heretic? Church leaders like Irenaeus would surely have said so, since he describes even milder dissidents as driven mad by Satan's wiles.[8] Or does this portrait of "the twelve" disciples and their followers point to issues so important that Christians on both sides were ready to consign one another to hell? Unlike other disagreements raging in the early church, this one clearly split communities apart. Indeed, the author portrays a dispute that has become deadly, for "the twelve" are said to stone Judas.

What lies behind these polarizing accusations? After working on the *Gospel of Judas* for some time, we came to see that we cannot easily dismiss this author either as a madman or a heretic. When we place the gospel in the context of what we know about Christians in the second century, the period when the *Gospel of Judas* was written, we can see him as a Christian who takes a strong — and, ultimately, losing — stance on an issue that intensely engages Christians at his time: the continuing persecution of Jesus's followers at the hands of the Romans.

In its beginning, Christianity consisted of a small and obscure set of groups that did not draw much attention from the Romans. Followers of Jesus met in homes and apparently had relatively little public presence at all. The actual persecutions were local and sporadic, depending much upon the attitudes of local communities and the inclinations of Roman magistrates. But despite these small numbers, Christians were not safe until 313, when the emperor Constantine, following his own conversion, ordered that all religions be tolerated. Until that time, because they refused to sacrifice to Rome's gods, they were regarded as atheists and traitors. Those who worshipped the Roman gods associated sacrifice with fundamental social virtues: obedience to the gods, civic and imperial loyalty, family duty, peace, and prosperity. The most prominent sacrifices were great public occasions, involving processions, prayers, omens, and festive meals, as well as the actual slaughter and offering of the victims, and these could be major political events, especially when the sacrifices were offered on behalf of the Roman emperor as a sign of loyalty and support. To refuse to support the Roman gods, then, was potentially an act of rebellion against Rome itself. Thus, if Christians came to the attention of the authorities, they were liable to be tortured or savagely killed as atheists or traitors to Rome.

Although not many people, numerically speaking, were arrested and executed in the first and second centuries, every believer was no doubt acutely aware of the danger and had to consider what to do if caught and accused. The situation deteriorated dramatically in the third century (249–252 C.E.), when the emperor Decius instituted a systematic attempt to force Christians to prove their loyalty by requiring everyone to make a sacrifice to the gods, and to prove they had done so by obtaining a receipt called a *libellus.* In the early fourth century (303–305 C.E.), the emperor Diocletian ordered everyone to sacrifice or face death. These violent attempts to wipe out Christianity were short-lived — and ultimately unsuccessful — but they etched sharp images onto the collective psyche of Christians, who up to the present day tell stories glorifying the heroic faith of the early martyrs.[9]

Like every Christian of his time, the author of the *Gospel of Judas* knew that becoming a Christian was dangerous. Wherever persecution flared up, fear must have permeated the lives of those who belonged to the movement.[10] Tertullian, whose North African community was being targeted in the early third century, tells how threats of violence shadowed Christians everywhere as soldiers and magistrates burst into gatherings where they met for worship, seeking the leaders, scattering the terrified worshippers, and threatening arrest.[11] Situations like these sparked heated debate among believers about how to react. What was a believer to do? A few suggested that one should say whatever necessary to survive, arguing that "Christ died for us so that we would live."[12] But most agreed that if accused, they would have to admit that they were Christians rather than offer sacrifice to the Roman gods, since Jesus had warned that "whoever denies me before others, I also will deny before my Father in heaven" (*Matthew* 10:32–33). Some teachers, then, including the famous second-century teacher Heracleon, later branded a heretic, recommended that believers not *volunteer* that they were Christians, but if asked, they should "confess Christ" and take the consequences — even disgrace and torture, often followed by agonizing, and spectacular, public execution.[13]

Yet other situations were more ambiguous. What if they knew the Romans were coming? Should they flee? — as Jesus had told his disciples: "When they persecute you in one town, flee to the next; for truly, I say to you, you will not have gone through all the towns of Israel before the Son of Man comes" (*Matthew* 10:23) — or was that a cowardly act that condemned them as thoroughly as if they had offered sacrifice? Was it acceptable to bribe officials in order to avoid that terrible moment where one had either to deny being a Christian or face torture and death? And what about extortionists? Should they pay money to silence people who threatened to inform on them? Here some cited Jesus's teaching to "Make friends for yourselves by means of dishonest wealth" (*Luke* 16:9). Sometimes, too, Christians were able to pay a ransom for those who had already confessed, and thus aid them in escaping martyrdom. Was such an act Christian charity or were they thwarting God's will?[14] We know these issues were being debated because Tertullian wrote the

83

treatise *On Fleeing Persecution* (C. 212 C.E.), in which he spoke about exactly these questions. While he offered some pragmatic advice, suggesting that Christians meet at night and only in small groups of three, so as not to attract notice, he firmly insisted that they should in no way try to avoid martyrdom. Everything that happens, he assures them, is according to God's will, which cannot be avoided in any case, but most important, martyrdom is God's will, for it glorifies God and strengthens the community of the faithful. One anonymous Christian even urges them to think of martyrdom as a great bargain: With the suffering of one hour, you can purchase for yourself eternal life![15]

To encourage their fellow believers to face death with courage, those who saw martyrs die wrote accounts of their astonishing courage. A famous one tells of an incident that occurred in the year 177 in rural France.[16] In the towns of Lyons and Vienne, Irenaeus, then a missionary from Syria, saw fellow believers attacked by hostile mobs; later, many were arrested and charged as atheists for failing to sacrifice to the gods of Rome. Although many who were arrested changed their minds when they faced sentences of torture and death, thirty to fifty stood firm and were chained in a dark, stinking prison to await public execution. Many died of exposure or torture in prison, and others were strangled; those who survived prison were killed with slow and excruciating torture in the town's sports arena on a day set aside for their townspeople to watch the spectacle. Perhaps ten years earlier, before these attacks on Christians in Gaul, Irenaeus had learned that his own beloved teacher and mentor, the venerable Polycarp, often called "the teacher of Syria," had been arrested, tried, and burned alive in the arena of the capital city.[17] Such deaths were seared into his memory. After he was ordained bishop to replace the ninety-year-old Pothinus, who had died in prison after being tortured, Irenaeus wrote to praise martyrs who, he said, "follow in the footsteps of the Lord" — and to denounce "heretics" who, he charged, failed to follow their example.[18]

Many other leaders of the church also tended to glorify deaths like these. While Roman magistrates saw such executions as necessary to secure the religious and political stability of their empire, Christians called those who died *martyrs* — that is, "witnesses" to the truth of Christ. For when Jesus's followers argued about what to do if arrested and what their deaths might mean, many reflected on how Jesus himself suffered and died.

Over the centuries, Jesus's followers have given many meanings to his suffering and death.[19] Some picture Jesus as the good shepherd who lays down his life for his sheep, showing God's love for humankind, as the *Gospel of John* says (*John* 10:11). Paul believed that Jesus's death turned the tide of history, making it possible for all to inherit the promises of salvation made to Israel (*Romans* 9–11). The rite of baptism was — and is — for many Christians a reenactment of Jesus's death and resurrection: going down into the water as a dying to the old life, rising up to the new life of the Spirit. Early Christians recognized, too, that Jesus's suffering put God on the side of the poor and oppressed, as liberation theologians have emphasized.

But like anyone bereaved by violence, some followers of Jesus expressed anger and imagined vengeance. The *Gospel of Luke* placed responsibility on the Jews — leading horribly to repeated violence against the Jewish people under the false notion that it was they, and not the Romans, who had killed Jesus.[20] Others aimed their anger at the Romans. The *Book of Revelation,* for example, pictures Jesus returning from heaven as a victorious warrior, leading an army of angels to kill his enemies and cast them into a lake of fire that burns forever. It describes Rome as a whore of "Babylon," dressed in imperial purple and sitting on seven hills — the famed hills of Rome — "drunk with the blood of the saints and the blood of the witnesses to Jesus" (*Revelation* 17:1–6). An angel assures John that God will give her over to the beast, who will "make her desolate and naked," devouring her flesh and burning her up with fire (*Revelation* 17:16). The author of the *Gospel of Judas,* too, is angry — but his anger is not aimed at Jews or Romans but at his fellow Christians, and he has Jesus firmly condemn them: "Truly I say to you, no race from the people among you will ever know me" (*Judas* 2:11).

Why this anger? Judas not only accepts Jesus's death, he helps facilitate it, even though he knows that this action seals his own violent death. So the problem for the author of the *Gospel of Judas* is not simply resistance to martyrdom. He does not criticize the martyrs themselves, nor does he say that dying as a martyr is a bad thing. Rather, he is angry at the *meaning* other Christians give to the deaths of Jesus and his followers, targeting those who claim that God desired Jesus's death as a sacrifice that God not only wills but commands.[21] For some Christians contemplating their own deaths came to understand Jesus's death — and their own — as sacrifice. As they struggled to come to terms with his death what dominated the imagination of some of his earliest followers, including the author of the *Gospel of Judas,* was the slaughter of animals in sacrifice. Animal sacrifice, an act that the majority of people throughout the Roman empire took for granted as the central act of public religious devotion, was always a bloody display, even though animals were killed with a single blow and then butchered to provide meat for the feast — but only after priests had pulled out their internal organs to look for omens.[22] Though the Temple in Jerusalem had been destroyed by the time the *Gospel of Judas* was written, the author pictures the disciples acting like priests in the Temple.

Images of Jesus are scattered throughout early Christian literature. Paul adopts an earlier Christian confession that "Christ died for our sins" (*I Corinthians* 15:3), and once he pictures Jesus as "our pascal lamb, Christ, (who) has been sacrificed" (*I Corinthians* 5:7), associating his death with the

Passover slaughter of lambs whose throats were cut at the altar of the great Temple in Jerusalem before the priests offered the corpses as sacrifices to God.[23] Those who wrote the New Testament *Gospels of Matthew* and *Mark* believed that Jesus, the night before his death, had envisioned his own death as sacrifice, telling the disciples that his own blood was to be "poured out for many, for the forgiveness of sins" (*Matthew* 26:28) and that he came "to give his life as a ransom for many" (*Mark* 10:45). A similar image dominates the *Gospel of John,* which identifies Jesus from the moment he first appears as "the lamb of God who takes away the sins of the world" (*John* 1:29). When the author of the *Gospel of John* narrates the crucifixion, he even changes the usual account of the story to show Jesus dying at the time when the Passover lambs were being slaughtered, and describes the crucifixion in language that echoes traditional biblical instructions for preparing the lamb to be eaten at the Passover meal (*John* 19:14). It is the author of the *Letter to the Hebrews,* however, who most fully depicts Jesus's death as a sacrifice, describing in livid detail how Christ "not with the blood of goats and calves, but with his own blood" secured redemption. The author explains that if animal blood and ashes purify people's defiled flesh, then how much more will Christ's offering of his own blood purify people to worship "the living God" (*Hebrews* 9:12–14). It is this kind of thinking that horrified the author of the *Gospel of Judas*.

But Jesus's followers took this image even further as they taught others to celebrate ritually a community meal to reenact Jesus's sacrificial death. Paul quotes Jesus and then tells his readers that "as often as you eat this bread and drink the cup, you proclaim the Lord's death until he comes" (*I Corinthians* 11:26). The *Gospel of John* goes further, having Jesus declare that "unless you eat the flesh of the Son of Man and drink his blood, you have no life in you. Those who eat my flesh and drink my blood have eternal life, and I will raise them up on the last day; for my flesh is true food and my blood is true drink" (*John* 6:53–55).

Yet the *Gospel of John* also tells us that this statement — smacking of cannibalism — was so offensive that many followers of Jesus left because of it. Here we get the first hint that this interpretation of Jesus's death might be the reason why Judas handed Jesus over, for it was this issue already in the *Gospel of John* that led Jesus to separate

Judas from "the twelve" and mark him as a betrayer (*John* 6:64–71). And yet Jesus's response here to those who desert him sounds amazingly similar to the teaching of Jesus in the *Gospel of Judas:*

> "Does this offend you? Then what if you were to see the Son of Man ascending to where he was before? It is the spirit that gives life; the flesh is useless. The words that I have spoken to you are spirit and life" (*John* 6:61–63).

It may be that the author of the *Gospel of Judas* read this passage in the *Gospel of John,* and thought that Judas alone understood what Jesus really meant here, and that was why he handed Jesus over, following Jesus's command at the last supper (*John* 13:27). Other Christians misunderstood when they thought Judas was possessed by Satan.

What exactly did they misunderstand? In the *Gospel of Judas,* as well as the *Gospel of John,* Jesus taught that "the spirit gives life, but the flesh is useless." But many of Jesus's followers would come to believe that suffering was required for salvation, and these understood their own suffering as a sacrifice to God, an imitation of the sacrificial death of Jesus.

Many of Jesus's followers, aware that they too might face violent death "for the sake of his name," saw their own sufferings — torture, abuse, pain, and death — as ways of "following Christ." Paul declared that he himself had given up everything, and was prepared to give up his life:

> I want to know Christ and the power of his resurrection and the sharing of his sufferings by becoming like him in his death, if somehow I may attain the resurrection from the dead (*Philippians* 3:10–11).

Thus Paul had assured believers that suffering for Jesus unites his followers with him, and ensures that they too shall be raised from the dead and welcomed in heaven.

No one speaks more radically to this desire to "die for God" than Ignatius, the bishop of Antioch in Asia Minor, whom the Roman authorities arrested around 115 C.E. While a hostile band of soldiers transported him to Rome for execution, Ignatius wrote letters to Christian congregations along the route, and sent one famous letter ahead to believers in Rome to urge them to "pray Christ for me that by these means I may become God's sacrifice" (Ignatius *Romans* 4:2), insisting that being torn apart by wild animals in the public arena would let him "attain to God" and ensure his salvation.

Speaking as if martyrdom were the best — if not the only — way to "gain God," Ignatius insisted that the wild beasts would offer him great opportunity to "imitate the suffering of my God" (by which, of course, he meant Jesus; Ignatius *Romans* 6:4). Ignatius envisioned his own body, like Jesus's body, becoming "God's bread" to be eaten as a eucharist: "I am God's wheat, and I am ground by the teeth of wild beasts to make a pure loaf for Christ" (Ignatius *Romans* 4:1). Ignatius prayed that nothing interfere with his plan:

Let there come upon me fire, and cross, and agony with wild beasts, racking of bones, mangling of limbs, crushing of my whole body — only let me attain to Christ Jesus! (Ignatius *Romans* 5:3).

Other Christians wrote accounts extolling the martyrs as heroes, both to encourage believers to stand firm and to impress unbelievers with the steadfastness of Christian faith. Such leaders carefully preserved many writings that glorify martyrdom, and

Christians still read them. One famous account, *The Acts of Justin and His Companions,* for example, imaginatively reconstructs the scene of how a Christian philosopher was put on trial in Rome C. 165 C.E. In it, Justin, the converted philosopher (known as Saint Justin Martyr) was arrested along with six of his students, men and women, who had gathered in his Rome apartment to hear him teach "Christian philosophy." All seven, we are told, were arraigned before Rusticus, city prefect of Rome, who, to test their loyalty to Rome, ordered them to sacrifice to the gods. But often the accused refused to answer questions, instead repeating loudly that "we are Christians"; and all refused the judge's order. Perplexed and frankly curious at their vehemence, even after he had threatened them with execution, Rusticus turned to Justin: "You are said to be educated, and you think you know what is true. Now listen: if you are whipped and beheaded, do you think you will go up into heaven? . . . Do you suppose that you will go up into heaven, and receive valuable rewards?" Justin answered, "I do not *suppose* it; but I *know* it clearly, and am entirely certain." When the others, too, again refused to offer sacrifice, Rusticus pronounced the sentence — whipping, then beheading. As Justin and the others filed out of the courtroom, the Christian author has them loudly praising God, perhaps in words like those spoken by other Christians receiving the death penalty: "Thanks be to God! Today we are martyrs in heaven."[24]

Yet some people expressed reservations, even revulsion. Some pagan spectators who watched members of Irenaeus's congregations die on that August day in 177 C.E. were heard to ask, "What good did their religion do them?"[25] Leaders like Irenaeus and Tertullian, who had seen persecution firsthand, believed that the survival of the movement was at stake — and they may have been right. Tertullian boasted to one Roman magistrate in North Africa that killing Christians only increases fervor while inspiring more people to join them: "The more you mow us down, the more we multiply; the blood of the martyrs is seed" for the church.[26] When certain Christians questioned the value of martyrdom, Irenaeus denounced them as "heretics," while Tertullian mocked them as cowards.[27] And when the fourth-century churchman Eusebius chronicled the history of the churches up to the time of Constantine, he gave pride of place to martyrs as the foundation of the church, describing them as great heroic saints whose courage and faith testified to the truth with their tortured bodies. So successful was this campaign to make heroes of the martyrs that any dissent was drowned out almost completely.

And yet we now know that some Christians reacted with anger, vociferously objecting when others glorified martyrdom. The stakes were high, and the arguments intense. What we hear in the *Gospel of Judas* is a sharp, dissenting voice. And that author's voice was not the only one; other dissenters speak through additional texts that were suppressed and eventually buried at Nag Hammadi, from the *Testimony of Truth* to the *Apocalypse of Peter;* no doubt others were lost. But as we have seen, since those whom later tradition enshrined as "fathers of the church" all stood on the other side of this issue, the only voices that were preserved were of those like Irenaeus, who dismissed works such as the *Gospel of Judas* that challenged their stand on martyrdom as "an abyss of madness, and blasphemy against Christ."[28] Because we hear next to nothing about such Christians, we might think that not many — or very few — actually did object, since virtually everything that dissidents wrote was scattered and lost. But now the discovery of the *Gospel of*

Judas, along with earlier discoveries, allows us to hear, for the first time in nearly two thousand years, a few voices of those who dissented. And we can now see why they objected. Above all, they raise two questions: What does such teaching say about God? And how does it impel people to act?

CHAPTER THREE:
SACRIFICE AND THE LIFE OF THE SPIRIT

The author of the *Gospel of Judas* draws his wild caricature of "the twelve" as priests at the altar, leading multitudes astray and offering human sacrifice, in order to point out what he feels is a stunning contradiction: that while Christians refuse *to practice sacrifice, many of them bring sacrifice right back into the center of Christian worship — by claiming that Jesus's death is a sacrifice for human sin, and then by insisting that Christians who die as martyrs are sacrifices pleasing to God.* Had this author seen church leaders encouraging others — perhaps young men or women he knew, perhaps even members of his own family — to embrace death in this way? Of course we have no way of knowing, but his writing conveys the urgency of someone who wants to unmask what he feels is the hideous folly of religious leaders who encourage people to get themselves killed this way — as though their suffering would guarantee the martyrs' personal resurrection to huge rewards in heaven, just as Justin declared to the Roman judge who sentenced him.

Yet the *Gospel of Judas,* too, pictures Jesus's death as a sacrifice, for he tells Judas that by handing him over, he will surpass them all, for "you will sacrifice the human being who bears me" (*Judas* 15:4). So even though Jesus tells the disciples to "cease sac[rificing]" (*Judas* 5:17), the issue for the *Gospel of Judas* is not simply whether Jesus's death and the deaths of his fellow Christians should be understood as sacrifices — he agrees that they should. But what he thinks is wrong is when bishops like Ignatius and Irenaeus teach that those who "perfect" themselves through a martyr's death are ensuring that God will reward them by raising them physically from the dead — they are wrong both in the "God" they worship and in thinking that the physical body will be raised to eternal life.

These errors arise because people are unable to perceive that anything exists beyond this mortal, visible world; they are unable to understand their place in the divine scheme of things. Because of this ignorance, the true God and Father sent Jesus to teach and heal so that people could come to know what "no human will see" and "whose measure no angelic race has comprehended" (*Judas* 10:1,2). He teaches Judas that there is a wider universe of the spirit beyond the limited world people perceive, and unless they come to know it, they will never know God or fulfill their own spiritual nature. For there is another glorious divine realm above the material world, and an immortal holy race exists above the perishable human race: these, he says, are "the mysteries of the kingdom" (*Judas* 9:20). As long as they remain ignorant, people are easy prey to the error of false gods. But Jesus appeared on earth in order to show the true nature of the universe and the end time so that those who understand these things would turn away from the worship of false gods — with all its sacrificial violence and immorality — and discover their true spiritual nature.

Almost half of Jesus's teaching is taken up with instructing Judas about the existence and structure of the heavenly realm above, about how this world and the gods who rule it came into being, and about what will happen at the end of time. He teaches him that the supposed "God" whom the other disciples worship is merely a lower angel who is leading them astray by impelling them to offer bloody sacrifice. It is this false "God"

who is responsible for having Jesus killed —
and his disciples prove they are just like him
when they blaspheme Jesus and stone Judas
to death.

As the *Gospel of Judas* opens, Jesus finds
his disciples praying and giving thanks as
they bless bread for worship — but he
laughs at them for what they are doing.
What, then, is wrong with their worship?
What provokes Jesus's contempt? What the
disciples are doing is probably not simply
offering thanks over a shared meal but
practicing the "thanksgiving" over the bread
that Christians called *"eucharist,"* to "proclaim the Lord's death," as the apostle Paul
had taught (*I Corinthians* 11:23–26).[1] Jesus
explains to them that he is not mocking
them; he's laughing because they don't
understand that they are practicing the eucharist "so that your 'God' will receive
praise." They wrongly think that Jesus is the
son of their "God" (*Judas* 2:6–9) and refuse
to hear what he is saying, comfortable in
their self-righteousness: "[This] is what is
right," they protest (*Judas* 2:5).

As we saw, when Jesus tries to instruct the
disciples, all but Judas resist him, getting
angry when he scoffs at their pieties, and
blaspheming him — proving that their "God
who is within you" is easy to provoke (*Judas*

2:12–15). Only Judas is able to stand before Jesus, even though he is not able to look him in the eyes but turns his face aside. But although he averts his eyes, Judas recognizes who Jesus is, and dares speak: "I know who you are, and which place you came from" (*Judas* 2:16–22). Thus Judas demonstrates that he is capable of comprehending what the vision reveals — that beyond the universe we perceive with our senses lies an invisible realm of Spirit that we must come to know in order to know God, and our own spiritual nature.

Jesus then takes Judas aside and begins to teach him privately what the others are not yet ready to hear: that beyond the visible world they know is a heavenly realm where a great invisible Spirit dwells in an infinite cloud of light. Although surpassing description, this creative energy is the divine source of all things, both those in heaven and those on earth. He teaches Judas that God first created the invisible, heavenly realm, filling it with divine beings, lights, and eternal realms called *aeons,* each with countless myriads of angels.

In contrast to this brilliant eternal realm of light, the visible world we live in now exists only as a kind of primeval darkness and disorder. Before God created the cosmos, in the beginning there was only chaos — like the description in *Genesis* 1:2 that "the earth was a formless void and darkness covered the face of the deep." According to the author of the *Gospel of Judas,* God in his goodness brought light and order to this world by setting rulers over it in the form of the heavenly bodies — just as *Genesis* 1:14–19 describes God creating "lights" in the dome of the sky to rule the seasons and illumine the earth. Jesus also reveals to Judas the names of the rulers God ordained: Nebro (Ialdabaoth), Saklas, and other angels. They are clearly associated with specific heavenly bodies: the sun with Nebro (with his face of fire), the seven-day week with Saklas and his six angels, the zodiac with the twelve angels (who are each given a portion of heaven), and the angels set to rule over "the chaos and the oblivion" with the five planets (*Judas* 12:5–21).

Confusing as this account might appear to the modern reader, it is crucial because it explains how evil, injustice, and suffering came to exist in a world created by a loving and all-powerful God. This conviction — that, far from being chaotic or random, the universe was constructed by God according to a harmonious order — is expressed in what is probably the original meaning of the Greek term *cosmos* ("order"). But the author of the *Gospel of Judas* suggests that the term also means "what perishes." That double meaning expresses the view that God's creation is good but that nonetheless the rulers of the lower world are flawed beings, who can lead humanity astray. Jesus explains that God's goodness consists in ordering and illuminating the primeval darkness of chaos; but nonetheless, in order for the angels He creates to be able to rule over this world, they have to partake of the nature of the world they rule. That means that they are limited in power and understanding; theirs is the dim and consuming light of fire, not the glory of divine illumination. In this way, Jesus's teaching here accounts for how "fallen angels" come to have dominion over the world — much like Satan and his angels, who appear in other Christian works such as the *Book of Revelation* in the New Testament, exercise sway over the world.

As in the *Book of Revelation,* the *Gospel of Judas* teaches that God has set a limit to the time that these lower angels will rule. At the end time, the lesser heavenly beings will be destroyed, along with the stars and planets and the people they lead astray. The author of the *Gospel of Judas* agrees with the *Gospel of Mark* that when the end time comes, what God created "in the beginning" will collapse: "(T)he sun will be darkened, and the moon will not give its light, and the stars will be falling from heaven, and the powers in the heavens will be shaken" (*Mark* 13:24–25). For many Christians, then as now, believed that the end time would be a time of judgment, when those who do evil and the spiritual powers that incite them to do evil will be destroyed. So, too, Jesus teaches Judas that when the time of Saklas's rule comes to an end, the stars will bring everything to completion, just as he prophesies; and all those people who worship the angels will fall into a moral abyss, fornicating and killing their children (*Judas* 14:2–8) — these are the signs of the end.

What is most striking, however, is that in all the Christian literature we know, only the author of the *Gospel of Judas* says that those who commit these sins do so in Jesus's name — that they are "Christians!" When people like "the twelve" practice eucharist and sacrifice and encourage others to follow their lead, they have fallen under the influence of angels who themselves err, leading astray the people who worship them into error and suffering. For as the *Gospel of*

Judas explains, although these angels were created and appointed by God, they are deficient beings. Unlike the heavenly angels in the divine realm above, they are mortal, limited in their understanding, and sometimes make mistakes. This suggestion is not original to the author of the *Gospel of Judas:* Other Jewish and Christian sources of the time also introduce such angels into the creation story to help account for the sufferings and mistakes that characterize much of human experience — while at the same time exempting God from creating anything evil.

Those who fall under such sinister celestial influences may be driven, like "the twelve," to commit violence and sexual immorality — even killing their own children in the name of some lesser heavenly power they mistake for God. As we have seen, Jesus rebukes "the twelve" for making such a mistake — a fatal one, because, he teaches, the way a person envisions God affects the way one lives. What was wrong with "the twelve" was that they *believed* they worshipped the God who was Jesus's Father but mistakenly imagined that "their God" required sacrifice — not only the death of Jesus but also the "sacrificial" death of their wives and children, who no doubt represent the martyrs of the author's own day whom church leaders encouraged to die for their faith. Even when they worship God, they "celebrate" their eucharist by reenacting a death — the crucifixion seen as sacrifice. When Jesus laughs at their worship, instead of asking him why or considering that they might be making a mistake, they angrily blaspheme him to his face. Thus their own angry violence mirrors that of "their God." But the reverse is also true: When Jesus reveals to Judas a different vision of God, this different vision creates within him and all who worship God a very different sense of who they are — and what God requires.

According to the *Gospel of Judas,* then, the fundamental problem is that "the twelve" — here, stand-ins for church leaders — do not know who Jesus is and do not understand who God is, either. They wrongly think that God requires suffering and sacrifice. But the author of the *Gospel of Judas* — and others within the early movement as well — was asking questions like this: What does such teaching make of God? Is God, then, unwilling or unable to forgive human transgression without violent bloodshed — from either the cut throats of goats and bulls, or — worse — human sacrifice?[2] Are Christians to worship a God who demands what the Hebrew Bible says that the God of Abraham refused — child sacrifice, even that of his own son? What kind of God would require anyone — much less his own son — to die in agony before he accepts his followers?

Over the centuries, Christians have answered these questions in various ways.[3] One answer is that God is, of course, merciful and loving but also just in requiring sacrifice to atone for human sin: Somehow, the debt incurred by sin must be paid. But the measure of his love, as the *Gospel of John* says, is precisely this — that "God so loved the world that he gave his only son, so that everyone who believes in him may not perish but may have eternal life" (*John* 3:16). What could demonstrate God's love more fully than that?

Yet the *Gospel of Judas* and other newly discovered works show that some Christians argued instead that people are gravely mistaken in worshipping such a limited, angry — even cruel — "God." As we saw, when Jesus mocks his disciples' eucharist, the author of the *Gospel of Judas* says they do not realize that they worship in error — not the true God but, as Jesus tells them, "your 'God.'" Astonished, the disciples protest that "*you* are the Son of our God," but they are wrong. Jesus is the son of the true God. The *Gospel of Judas* pictures such worship as a nightmare — one that distorts Jesus's teaching, mistakes the meaning of his death, and gives a false picture of God.

Ingeniously, the *Gospel of Judas* pictures the nightmare as something that the twelve disciples themselves have dreamed up — and it goes on to dramatize their horror at what they dreamed. The disciples, it says, all had the same dream in which they saw twelve priests standing at a great altar offering sacrifice. But instead of picturing a scene of holy worship, they see these priests engaged in sacrilege — not only leading animals to sacrifice on their altar, but committing violence and sexual sin: above all, killing their own wives and children as human sacrifice, and doing all this in Jesus's name! Horrified, the disciples go to Jesus to tell him the dream and ask him what it could mean (*Judas* 4:2–17).

Jesus's answer shocks them even more: "You," he says, "are the twelve men whom you saw" (*Judas* 5:3). What they see in their dream is a graphic picture of what they themselves are doing. While imagining that they are pleasing God, they are actually serving their own distorted view of a "God" who, they believe, wants human sacrifice

(*Judas* 5:13–14). In their dream, they are seeing themselves as the true God sees them — as evil priests who lead many of their "flock" to their destruction, like animals to slaughter.

The *Gospel of Judas* does not tell us how the twelve disciples reacted, but if their previous behavior is any guide, they must have been horrified. Certainly the charge Jesus makes would have surprised and offended most readers, for Christians prided themselves on having rejected the practice of sacrifice, associating it either with Jewish worship in the Jerusalem Temple or with the worship of the false gods of their pagan neighbors. Praying and sacrificing to idols, they believed, would inevitably lead to immorality. Paul claims that people who do such things deserve to die (*Romans* 1:18–32) — and that the "gods" who require animal sacrifice, are really demons (*I Corinthians* 10:20).[4]

Yet Christians were not the first to denounce such practices. On the contrary, they were following traditions already well established in their day. Israel's prophets, as well as Greek and Roman philosophers, had criticized conventional religion for promoting superstition, immorality, and violence by giving people wrong ideas about God.

For centuries, Jewish teachers had denounced pagan worship, accusing their neighbors of carving images from wood or casting them from metal and then kneeling down to worship what they had made. Jewish teachers, including Jesus's disciple Paul, charged that devotion to false gods — gods who, they said, are actually demons[5] — leads people into violence, sexual immorality, perhaps even murder and the killing of children.[6]

The great Jewish prophets such as Amos, Hosea, and Isaiah denounced not only pagan worship but also the sacrifices offered by their own people to the one true God in the Jerusalem Temple. Speaking in the Lord's name, Hosea declared that "I desire steadfast love and not sacrifice, the knowledge of God, rather than burnt-offerings" (*Hosea* 6:6). Amos, too, speaking for God, declared:

> I hate, I despise your festivals. . . . Even though you offer me your burnt-offerings and grain-offerings, I will not accept them; and the offerings of well-being of your fatted animals I will not look upon. . . . But let justice roll down like waters, and righteousness like an ever-flowing stream (*Amos* 5:21–24).

111

Many Jews, including Jesus, agreed with Amos that what God requires above all is "to do justice, and to love kindness, and to walk humbly with your God" (*Micah* 6:8); without these virtues, sacrifice was unacceptable. According to the *Gospel of Mark,* Jesus teaches that the greatest commandment is to "love the Lord your God with all your heart, and with all your soul, and with all your mind. The second is this, 'You love your neighbor as yourself' " (*Mark* 12:30–31). After he speaks, a Jewish scribe applauds, agreeing that these commandments are "more important than all whole burnt-offerings and sacrifices" (*Mark* 12:33).[7]

Greek and Roman philosophers, too, criticized certain religious practices, arguing that their own myths about jealous and petty gods who fomented war and committed rape proved that these gods did not deserve devotion.[8] Some people even questioned whether slaughtering animals in sacrifice actually pleased the gods.[9] Philosophers often argued that the gods do not require the smell and taste of sacrifice for their food but rather, as the moral philosopher Porphyry said, "The best sacrifice to the gods is a pure mind and a soul free from passions."[10]

Yet everyone who criticized sacrifice —

whether Jew, Christian, or pagan — regarded human sacrifice as the worst of all. The Jewish author of the *Wisdom of Solomon,* for example, claimed that God gave the land of Canaan to the Israelites because the Canaanites had mercilessly slaughtered children, and feasted on the human flesh and blood they had sacrificed (*Wisdom* 12:5–6). The Roman governor Pliny says that the Senate first passed a law against human sacrifice only as recently as 97 B.C.E., and until then "these monstrous rites were still performed."[11] Pliny adds that suspect people — Druids and magicians — still practice human sacrifice; for him this proves how savage they are.[12] Whether accurate or not, these denunciations show that human sacrifice horrified people.

Since Christians were famous — or notorious — for rejecting sacrifice, and some even chose to die rather than perform it, the author of the *Gospel of Judas* surely intends to shock his readers when he pictures "the twelve" not only offering animals in sacrifice to God but offering him even human sacrifice! Only their worst enemies accused Christians of slaughtering children and promoting all kinds of immoral behavior. Some apparently understood the symbolic Christian practice of eating the body and drinking the blood of Jesus as, literally, cannibalism.[13]

Until recently it appeared that criticizing Christians for immorality came solely from the outside — notably, from Greek and Roman philosophers, who were appalled at this new "sect." The *Gospel of Judas* now adds a new voice to the bitter debate that was raging within Christian circles, like that of another outspoken Christian, who wrote a vehement attack he called the *Testimony of Truth* to challenge what he felt was the false testimony of those who glorified martyrdom. Like the *Gospel of Judas,* this protest was buried centuries ago; it was discovered only in 1945 near Nag Hammadi.[14] This author declares that "foolish people, thinking in their heart that if they only confess in words, 'We are Christians,' . . . while giving themselves over to a human death," they will gain eternal life. These "empty martyrs . . . testify only to themselves." What their actions really testify to, the author says, is their ignorance: "they do not know . . . who Christ is," and they foolishly believe that "if we deliver ourselves over to death for the sake of the name" — the name of Christ — "we will be saved." The author of the *Testimony of Truth,* like the author of *Judas,* suggests that such people do not know the true God. Those who imagine that human sacrifice pleases God have no understanding of the Father; instead, they have fallen under the influence of wandering stars that lead them astray (*Testimony of Truth* 34:1–11). Rather than turning believers toward salvation, such leaders actually are delivering them into the clutches of the authorities, who kill them. All that such violence accomplishes is their own destruction.

What, then, is "the true testimony" to Christ? To proclaim his mighty works of deliverance and compassion — how the Son of Man raised the dead, healed the paralyzed, restored sight to the blind, healed those suffering from sickness or tormented by demons. While these would-be martyrs are themselves "sick, unable to raise even themselves" (*Testimony of Truth* 31:22–34:11), this author declares that those who truly witness to Christ proclaim that God's power brings wholeness and life. The true testimony, this author declares, is "to know oneself, and the God who is over the truth." Only one who testifies to this message of deliverance wins the "crown" that others mistakenly say that martyrs earn by dying (*Testimony of Truth* 44:23–45:6).

While the *Testimony of Truth* thus denounces — even ridicules — the martyrs themselves, the *Gospel of Judas,* as we noted, stops short of this, choosing only to criticize the leaders who encourage would-be martyrs to court destruction. Another of the Nag Hammadi texts, the *Apocalypse of Peter,* allows us to hear the voice of a third vocal critic of Christian leaders who urge martyrdom upon devout believers. This author singles out especially "those who call themselves bishops and deacons, as if they had received their authority from God"; such people, he wrote, "are dry canals!" (*Apocalypse of Peter* 79:22–31). Charging that these leaders themselves are the heretics (*Apocalypse of Peter* 74:20–22), the *Apocalypse* says that "These are the ones who oppress their brothers, saying to them, 'Through this (suffering) our God has mercy, since salvation comes to us through this,' " oblivious that they themselves will incur divine punishment for the part they played in sending so many of the "little ones" to their death (*Apocalypse of Peter* 79:11–21).

When denouncing such leaders as not only mistaken but implicated in bloodshed, however, this author apparently is writing to fellow Christians who are living in fear of persecution. The *Apocalypse of Peter* — that

116

is, God's "revelation" to Peter — opens to a scene of Peter and other disciples standing in the Jerusalem Temple in a moment of mortal terror. Peter says, "I saw the priests and the people running up to us with stones, as if they would kill us; and I was afraid that we were doing to die" (*Apocalypse of Peter* 72:6–9). But instead of advising them to avoid suffering a martyr's death, the *Apocalypse of Peter* encourages them to face such a death with courage and hope, as Jesus tells Peter: "You, therefore, be courageous and do not fear at all. For I shall be with you in order that none of your enemies may prevail over you. Peace be to you. Be strong!" (*Apocalypse of Peter* 84:6–11). Thus the reader would understand that a writing like this, which claims to convey a "revelation" Jesus gave to Peter when the terrified disciple faced his own death, was also written to console any believer who feared the same fate — and, for that matter, anyone who faces, and fears, impending death.

When it comes to our second question — How does such teaching impel people to act? — some Christians, like Irenaeus, when faced with the reality of persecution and death, advocated that people should be martyred, arguing that God wills all this suffering for people's own good. For Irenaeus, suffering and even death are meant to teach people about the greatness and goodness of God in granting eternal life to a sinful humanity.[15] But the author of the *Gospel of Judas* not only denies that God desires such sacrifice, he also suggests that the practical effect of such views is hideous: It makes people complicit in murder. By teaching that Jesus died in agony "for the sins of the world" and encouraging his followers to die as he did, certain leaders send them on a path toward destruction — while encouraging them with the false promise that they will be resurrected from death to eternal life in the flesh.

But the *Gospel of Judas* rejects the resurrection of the body. What meaning, then, can be found in Jesus's death? The author offers a radical answer. When Jesus tells Judas to "sacrifice the human being who bears me," he is asking Judas to help him demonstrate to his followers how, when they step beyond the limits of earthly existence, they, like Jesus, may step into the infinite — into God.

CHAPTER FOUR:
THE MYSTERIES OF THE KINGDOM

The *Gospel of Judas* does not stop with condemning erroneous views about God and sacrifice, or practices of eucharist and baptism. On the contrary, such criticism of mistaken church leaders marks only its beginning. From this point, this gospel goes on to show "divine mysteries" revealed only to Judas — about God, about Jesus and the divine source whence he comes, and about how he — and the disciple who follows him — may enter that spiritual reality.

Jesus teaches Judas that at death, the bodies of all human beings will perish — there is no resurrection of the flesh. Only the souls of the great and holy race will be lifted up when their spirits separate from them (*Judas* 8:3–4). At the beginning Judas does not really understand, for when he has a dream, Jesus laughs at him, a clear indication that Judas has made some error. But rather than dismissing Judas, Jesus promises to support him. He encourages Judas to speak about his distress when he dreamed that "the twelve" disciples were stoning and persecuting him. But Judas also had a vision of the heavenly Temple — a glorious vision of a great house filled with brilliant light, and, high above, dense green foliage (*Judas* 9:9–12). People would immediately recognize this as the infinite light in which God dwells — the house of God. That, of course, is what Jews called the Jerusalem Temple; but what Judas sees — in stark contrast to "the twelve's" dream about bloody sacrifice in the earthly Temple — is the spiritual reality beyond this world, the divine reality that Israel's prophets often described simply as "light," the glory of God's presence, at which humanly built "houses of God," from the Jerusalem Temple to the cathedral at Chartres, can only hint.

But when Judas asks to go there and join the distinguished elders who surround the divine presence, Jesus rebukes him: "Your star is leading you astray, Judas" (*Judas* 9:15). This shows that although only Judas, of "the twelve," caught a glimpse of what Jesus meant when he began to speak to them about the mysteries that are beyond the world — for Judas alone perceived that

Jesus came from the immortal realm above (*Judas* 2:22–23) — he still has not fully understood what Jesus is trying to tell him. No mortal is worthy to go there, Jesus insists, because that place is reserved for the holy ones — that is, for people who are no longer subject to the sun and moon and the other angels who rule over the realm of chaos. So even though Jesus has already told Judas that he is able to reach the immortal realm (*Judas* 2:27), the disciple still doesn't understand fully Jesus's most central teaching — that for human beings to gain eternal life, they have to perceive the deeper vision of God that emerges from within. That is why Jesus began by challenging the disciples "to bring forth the perfect human." Those who do so discover that they have within them spiritual resources of which they were unaware.

For in the process of bringing forth the perfect human, one becomes aware of the deeper meaning of the *Genesis* account, which tells how God created humankind:

Then God said, "Let us make humankind in our image, according to our likeness . . ." So God created humankind in his image, in the image of God he created them; male and female he created them" (*Genesis* 1:26–27).

If human beings are created in the image of the divine, why is this image so hard to perceive and why does it take such courage to discover? Here Jesus goes on to explain that creation "in the image" refers to our original, spiritual nature, hidden deep within what we seem to be as ordinary men and women. It is that original quality of human being that was created in the image of a spiritual being called Adamas, who dwells in the light, where the true God dwells, hidden even from the angels (*Judas* 11:1–2). The human Eve, too, is created after the image of the heavenly race — because, like Adamas, Eve is also a heavenly being — and it is she who most deeply represents humanity's spiritual nature. For within the luminous cloud of light where Adamas dwells on high there also dwelt Eve. In Greek her name ("Zoe") means "Life," drawing on the wordplay found in Hebrew, in which "Eve" means "life," as the *Genesis* account shows: "The man called his wife's name Eve, because she was the mother of all living" (*Genesis* 3:20). Here Jesus teaches that "the whole race" of humans should seek eternal life *in her name* (*Judas*

13:2–4). What this means for human beings now is that those who come to recognize their true nature are children of these *spiritual* parents — not children like Cain and Abel, enmeshed in the story of the first murder, but children who resemble the lesser-known one, Seth, whom *Genesis* says Eve bore to Adam as their third son:

> When God created humankind, he made them in the likeness of God . . . When Adam had lived one hundred thirty years, he became the father of a son in his likeness, according to his image, and named him Seth (*Genesis* 5:1, 3)

All humanity, then, belongs to "the incorruptible race of Seth" (*Judas* 11:5), since everyone is a child of Adam and Eve, created according to the likeness and the image of God.

Why, then, does Jesus speak of *two* kinds of human races? Why is it that not everyone automatically understands the spiritual nature? To help Judas understand, Jesus tells him that Saklas was the one who decreed that human beings should only live for a short time and then perish. People have been led astray and polluted with the foolish "wisdom" of the world (*Judas* 8:7), because the rulers of chaos and oblivion "lord it over them." They've come to believe that this life of the flesh, our present life in this world, is all that really exists. When they try to imagine eternal life, they imagine it only as living on forever in the flesh, just as Justin, Irenaeus, and Tertullian say. But Jesus insists they are wrong. Although the *Gospel of Judas,* like the New Testament gospels, says that Jesus's teaching offers a path to eternal life, the key to that path is not what happens to the physical body; it is understanding humanity's spiritual connection to God. Those who understand the deeper secrets of creation, aware that they are created "in the image" of the divine source, may come to dwell above in the realm of the Spirit.

Jesus explains to Judas that God did not abandon humanity to the lower angels but made sure that Adam and those with him learned that the image of God they carry deep within makes them superior to the rulers of chaos (*Judas* 13:16–17). Judas is astonished when he hears this. At first he can't believe it is true, but gradually he comes to understand what it means. Jesus explains that because everyone received a divine spirit, everyone can worship God truly. Those who do so free themselves from the power of the lower angels, so that when their physical bodies die, their souls — now joined with spirits of the great and holy race above — ascend to the heavenly realm above (*Judas* 8:2–4; 9:22; 13:12–15). Judas finally understands Jesus's teaching, so that this time he does not turn his eyes away, but he lifts up his eyes so that he sees the cloud of light, and he enters into it (*Judas* 15:15–19).

Yet the *Gospel of Judas,* like the New Testament gospels, shows that Jesus's teaching is not limited to words; he also teaches through what he does. What he reveals is not complete when he finishes speaking — but only when he dies. His death demonstrates that the death of the body is not the end of life, but only a step into the infinite.

But does the *Gospel of Judas,* then, teach resurrection — a term it never mentions? The answer depends on what *resurrection* is taken to mean. For here, as in the case of crucifixion, *Judas'*s author plunged into controversial discussions that engaged believers of his time, a question that still troubles many today: What happened *after* Jesus died?

That Jesus "rose from the grave" to new life is a fundamental theme of Christian teaching; certainly it is the most radical. For even though most people believed in eternal life, the insistence of certain Christians like Irenaeus that their bodies would be buried, decompose — and yet rise again at the appointed time — was met not only with disbelief but with horror.[1] Christians themselves were unclear about what kind of body this resurrected body would be. When Paul wrote about the resurrection, although his words are often mistaken as arguing for physical resurrection, he himself clearly says the opposite: "What I am saying, brothers and sisters, is this: flesh and blood cannot inherit the kingdom of God, nor does the perishable inherit the imperishable" (*I Corinthians* 15:50). Without claiming to understand exactly what happens, Paul acknowledges that resurrection is a mystery, in which, he says, "we will all be changed" from physical to spiritual existence (*I Corinthians* 15:51–53). Accounts in other New Testament writings give different accounts of Jesus's resurrection, since what mattered most to these writers was their conviction that Jesus was somehow still alive, and not to specify any particular way this may have happened. Thus the gospels include a wide range of stories about people who claimed to have seen Jesus alive after he died. Some suggest that they saw him in a vision. When, for example, Stephen is being stoned, he gazes into heaven and sees Jesus at the right hand of God (*Acts* 7:55–56). Others are ambiguous. For example, the disciples on the road to Emmaus didn't recognize Jesus for hours, and when they did he "vanished," leaving them with the conviction that somehow — spiritually — he was still alive (*Luke* 24:13–31). In the *Gospel of John,* Mary of Magdala is the first to encounter the risen Lord, but she initially mistakes him for the gardener; the disciples out fishing don't at first recognize him either (*John* 20:15; 21:4). How could such intimates not recognize him? Yet others claimed not only that they had seen him but that they had touched and felt his body, raised out of the grave back to life. Those who told such stories insisted that his resurrection was an actual physical event. The *Gospel of Matthew,* for example, says that the disciples take hold of Jesus's feet (*Matthew* 28:9). One story the *Gospel of Luke* tells says that when the disciples saw Jesus, they were astonished and terrified, naturally assuming that they were seeing a spirit. But, they said, Jesus challenged them: "Touch me and see; for a ghost does not have flesh and bones as you see that I have." Since they still did not believe he was physically present, he asked for something to eat, and as they watched in amazement, he ate a piece of broiled fish. The point is clear: No spirit could do that (*Luke* 24:37–43). But even in these cases, it is an unusual physicality, for Jesus seemingly walks through solid walls and locked doors, and asks not to be touched (*John* 20:17–19).

Concerned to show that Jesus was somehow alive, as we have seen, the gospel writers included the various reports they had heard, without creating a single coherent narrative. But the stories they told raised questions among readers who asked what *resurrection* actually meant. From the late first century through the second, as Christians discussed this question, certain leaders insisted on one single version, declaring that Christians "must" believe that Jesus rose bodily from the dead — what they called "the resurrection of the flesh."[2]

Christians who deny this, Ignatius wrote, make Jesus's death into a sham. "It's really *they* who are a sham!" he exclaimed. Jesus was really crucified and died, and was really raised from the dead — otherwise, he insists, I would be dying to no purpose (Ignatius *Trallians* 9–10). His own sacrificial death, like Jesus's death on the cross, is no spiritual metaphor but the reality of painful torture and dying. For those facing the possibility of martyrdom, views like those in the *Gospel of Judas* or the *Apocalypse of Peter* made no sense of their suffering — or Jesus's death. It clearly offended their sense of justice. Irenaeus insists that since suffering occurs in the body, the righteous should be rewarded in the body. Otherwise why does God allow his beloved children to suffer so?[3]

It is this kind of thinking that the author of the *Apocalypse of Peter* challenges. If God will grant us mercy only if we suffer, what kind of God is this? Such leaders are wrong, he claims, to teach "the little ones" that "good and evil are from one source" — the one God (*Apocalypse of Peter* 77:30–32). Instead he insists that Jesus came to free people from slavery and suffering, and to forgive the sins they had committed in error (*Apocalypse of Peter* 78:8–15).

What meaning, then, does Jesus's death have? Jesus shows Peter that he should not fear death, because what dies is only the mortal body, not the living spirit. To show him this, Peter is given a vision of Jesus's passion to prepare him to face his own suffering and death. The Savior reveals to Peter that if he perceives the crucifixion not with his physical ears and eyes but with spiritual apprehension, he will be able to perceive the truth. The one into whose hands and feet they drive the nails is only the fleshly part; the living Jesus is untouched by this suffering and death (*Apocalypse of Peter* 81:4–24).[4] Peter expresses astonishment, for in a kind of double vision, he seems to see one person being seized and nailed to the cross while another, joyful and laughing, stands nearby. When Peter asks Jesus what this means, Jesus explains that when the body suffers mortal agony, it releases "the Spirit filled with radiant light" (83:9–10). Human beings are not saved by dying as martyrs but only by accepting God's forgiveness and standing fast against those who teach error and violence.

Why do other Christians not see this? The author of the *Gospel of Judas* suggests that it is because they believe in the resurrection of the flesh. Yet Christians like this author, while rejecting the idea of bodily resurrection, do not reject life after death. On the contrary, they suggest other ways of envisioning what that life might be. The *Gospel of Philip,* for example, calls belief in resurrection of the flesh the "faith of fools." Resurrection, this gospel explains, far from being a single historical event in the past, refers instead to the way that Christ's presence can be experienced here and now. Thus, those who are "born again" in baptism, symbolically speaking, also are "raised from the dead" when they awaken to spiritual life. Another anonymous Christian teacher, asked by a student named Rheginos to explain resurrection, wrote in reply an interpretation of what Paul had taught. Although resurrection does not involve the physical body, the teacher tells Rheginos, it is indeed a reality:

> . . . do not think the resurrection is an illusion. It is no illusion, but it is the truth! Indeed, it is more fitting to say the world is an illusion, rather than the resurrection, which has come into being through our Lord the Savior, Jesus Christ (*Treatise on the Resurrection* 48:10–19).

Struggling to speak, as Paul had, of "mystery," this teacher suggests that resurrection is "the revelation of what is, and the transformation of things, and a transition into newness." Yet descriptions like these, he acknowledges, are only "the symbols and the images of resurrection"; Christ alone, he says, brings us into its reality (*Treatise on the Resurrection* 48:30–49:9).

We noted before that the *Testimony of Truth*

deplores Christians foolish enough to believe that if they die as martyrs, they are guaranteed salvation, thinking, the author says, that "(i)f we deliver ourselves over to death for the sake of (Christ's) name we will be saved." But while imagining, as Justin did, that they would be resurrected and rewarded as Jesus had been, the author of the *Gospel of Judas* insists that they are only precipitating themselves into violent death.

Yet the second-century Christians who wrote such "revelations" recognized that they, too, were living at a time when Christians were often killed for their faith. Even those who refused to glorify martyrdom, or even admit it is "God's will," recognized that they also lived under constant threat of arrest, torture, and execution at the hands of Roman magistrates. Those who put aside the idea that Jesus died as a necessary sacrifice for sin or that martyrs will be resurrected were still left, after all, with questions these teachings were meant to solve: How can one deal with suffering? What kind of meaning can be found — if any — in Jesus's suffering and death, or that of anyone else, including our own? Two writings found in the Tchacos Codex[5] — the same ancient book that contains the *Gospel of Judas* —

offer clear answers. Both the *First Apocalypse of James* and the *Letter of Peter to Philip* imagine scenes in which various apostles face imminent — and violent — death. Jesus gives them "revelations" about his own suffering and death that explain why they, too, must suffer and die.

The author of the *First Apocalypse of James,* for example, writes about Jesus speaking with James, telling him that just as he himself will be captured and killed, so will James be stoned. The story reports that James "was afraid, and wept; and he was very distressed." As he and Jesus sit down together upon a rock, Jesus proceeds to tell him what to do, and how to face the powers that threaten his life. As in the *Gospel of Judas,* Jesus reveals to him that he comes from a divine source, to which he will return. The Savior returns after the resurrection and reassures James that "[n]ever have I suffered in any way, nor have I been distressed. And this people has done me no harm."[6] Like in the *Gospel of Judas,* Jesus's death in the *First Apocalypse of James* is meant to free people from the power of the lower-world rulers. Your death, Jesus tells James, will deliver you from them.[7] He allows the crucifixion in order to expose the

133

world rulers, for when they try to seize him, he overpowers them — proving that they are powerless as well as wicked.[8] When James learns that death only means giving back "the weak flesh," he wipes away his tears and is comforted. Like Judas, James too must suffer and die, but both learn from Jesus's example that death releases the fetters that bind them to the unjust rulers.

Similarly, the *Letter of Peter to Philip* tells how the disciples gathered together on the Mount of Olives, where they prayed to Jesus, "Son of life, Son of immortality, who is in the light, Son, Christ of immortality, our Redeemer, give us power, for they seek to kill us" (*Letter of Peter to Philip* 134:2–9). Out of a great light shining across the mountain the voice of Jesus tells them that it is necessary for them to preach salvation to the world, but that when they do, they will suffer, because the powers that rule the world are against them. You "are fighting against the inner man," he tells them, but the Father "will help you as he has helped you by sending me" — stressing that death is only that of the fleshly body, not of the spirit.[9] They are comforted when he assures them that they need not be afraid, because "I am with you forever." In the end, Peter acknowledges that the Lord Jesus "is the author of our life," and they all go out filled with power, in peace, to preach and heal. For these Christians, the fact that Jesus had suffered and died meant that he knew what they were facing — and promised to be with them.

All three of these works from the Tchacos Codex, including the *Gospel of Judas,* stress that anyone who sets out on the spiritual path and criticizes the ignorant and wicked powers that rule the world will be persecuted and will suffer — as Jesus repeatedly tells Judas. When Judas asks what good this will do him, Jesus tells him that although people will curse him, in the end he will rule over them all when he turns upward to the holy race (*Judas* 9:26–30). The more Judas understands, the more he realizes that he will be cursed and reviled in this world for doing what Jesus orders him to do. Yet as the *First Apocalypse of James* and the *Letter of Peter to Philip* show, Jesus's disciples are called to teach and heal, and so to stand against the powers of the world — both those fallen angels in the heavens and the people who act like them, killing Jesus and stoning Judas.[10] Finally, although the *Gospel of Judas* does not encourage martyrdom, ironically — or better, paradoxically — it portrays Judas himself as the first martyr.

This gospel reveals that when Judas hands Jesus over, he seals his own fate. But he knows, too, that when the other disciples stone him, they kill only his mortal self. His spirit-filled soul has already found its home in the light world above. Although Christians may suffer and die when they oppose the powers of evil, the hope Christ brings will sustain them. These revelations offer courage and comfort to anyone who anticipates suffering and death — and so to everyone.

But how can such a gospel be *good news* — since that is what "gospel" means? The author of the *Gospel of Judas* implies that everyone has the power to surpass the angelic powers, because, as Jesus teaches Judas, it is only people themselves who keep the spirit confined within the flesh (*Judas* 13:14–15). By seeking the spirit within themselves, they can overcome the rulers of chaos and oblivion, see God, and enter the heavenly house of God above. And they can do this even as they live in this world. Just as both Jesus and Judas enter the luminous cloud while living on earth, so those who follow them may lead the life of the spirit and know God here and now. The body cannot confine the knowing spirit any more than can death, which is but the final release

136

to God. Just as every life seems to end in the tragedy of death, the *Gospel of Judas* ends as Judas hands Jesus over to the enemies who will kill him. As this gospel tells it, Judas knows that doing so — even at Jesus's request — will lead the other disciples to hate him and stone him to death. What makes this "good news," however, is what he has discovered through Jesus's teaching and his death: that what dies is only his mortal self, and that his soul, filled with the spirit, already recognizes its home in God.

In seeking a vision of God within, the *Gospel of Judas* takes its place alongside a wide variety of new discoveries from Egypt, written to transmit what they thought Jesus actually taught. Some took their initial inspiration from the *Gospel of John.* The *Secret Revelation of John,* for example, claims to reveal "mysteries" that the Savior gave to "John, his disciple . . . the brother of James, the sons of Zebedee" (*Secret Revelation of John* II.1:2–3).[11] This tells how John, grieving for Jesus, went to the Temple to worship. But after a Pharisee mocked him for allowing Jesus to deceive him and turn him away from traditional Jewish teaching, John could not bring himself to go inside. Instead, he turned away and walked into a solitary place in the desert, tormented with grief and doubt. Suddenly, John says, the earth shook and brilliant light blazed around him. Terrified, John then saw Christ appear in the light, changing forms, appearing first in the form of a child, then as an old man. He heard him speak: "John, John, why are you doubting and fearful? . . . I am the one who dwells with you always. I am the Father. I am the Mother. I am the Son" (*Secret Revelation of John* II.9:11–12). Just as in the *Gospel of Judas,* the Savior comforts John by instructing him about the whole universe, the truth of God, and the origin and salvation of humanity. As John's terror subsided, he came to see that the spiritual life the Savior embodied — and that he experienced within himself — lives; and with joyful relief John realized that this is the "light that shone in the darkness," and that darkness cannot overcome (cf. *John* 1:5).

Another gospel that Irenaeus knew and denounced, the *Gospel of Truth,* also began from reflection on what Paul and the *Gospel of John* had taught, that Jesus's death reveals God's love for us — but takes it in a different direction. Without contradicting the familiar teaching that Jesus's death atones for sin, this gospel opens by saying that "the gospel of truth is joy to those who have received from the Father of truth the grace of knowing him." Speaking of the "terror and fear" we feel when we live apart from God, it goes on to say that Jesus came into the world as a "hidden mystery" to bring light to all who were distressed and living in darkness (*Gospel of Truth* 18:15–18). But instead of a sacrifice offered for human sin, the *Gospel of Truth* pictures Jesus on the cross as "fruit on a tree" — like fruit on the tree of knowledge in *Genesis* 2:17. Through this image the *Gospel of Truth* transforms the meaning of the eucharist. For while eating from the tree of knowledge in Paradise "brought death" upon those who ate it, eating this true "fruit of the tree of knowledge" brings life. Thus the *Gospel of Truth* suggests that those who partake of Jesus, sharing in the bread that symbolizes his body, discover the "hidden mystery" — that is, their own connection with God. By participating in this intimate communion they come to know God — not through the intellect but through the knowledge of the heart — and to know one another. In this way, the *Gospel of Truth* says, "he discovered them in himself, and they discovered him in themselves" (*Gospel of Truth* 18:29–31).

Like a poet, the author of the *Gospel of*

Truth offers a second image of the cross. As in a dream, the cross becomes a wooden post on which imperial edicts are published for all to see. But what Jesus "published" on the cross was God's will. For as a will is opened only when someone dies, so through dying Jesus opened up God's will for everyone to see: ". . . Jesus appeared. He put on that book. He was nailed to a tree. He published the edict of the Father on the cross. O, such great teaching!" (*Gospel of Truth* 20:23–28). What Jesus "published," so to speak, was the names of all God's beloved children, and what God wills is simply this: that they all come to know and love him, and one another.

What kind of God, then, wills only this? Contradicting believers who warn of God's wrath and judgment, the *Gospel of Truth* declares that those who really know him "do not think of him as small, or harsh, or wrathful," as others suggest, but as a loving and gracious Father (*Gospel of Truth* 42:4–9). Poetic, sometimes lyrical, this gospel declares that God sent his son not only to save us from sins committed in error but to restore all beings to the divine source whence they came, "so that they may return to the Father and to the Mother, Jesus of the utmost sweetness" (*Gospel of Truth*

24:6–9). Thus to all who wander this world in terror, anguish, and confusion, Jesus reveals a divine secret: that they are deeply connected with God the Father, and with the divine Mother, the Holy Spirit. To those who experience life in this world as a nightmare, this message offers hope that "You are the perfect day, and in you dwells the light that does not fail" (*Gospel of Truth* 32:31–34).

A third interpretation of Christ's passion, inspired by the *Gospel of John,* is the remarkable poem called the *Round Dance of the Cross.*[12] The anonymous Christian who wrote this poem, noting that the *Gospel of John* never tells the story of the "last supper" in which Jesus tells his disciples to eat bread as his body and drink wine as his blood, apparently writes an episode to supply what is missing, and to suggest that something else happened that night. The *Acts of John* tells how, after dinner, Jesus led his disciples outdoors, and invited them to dance and sing with him:

Before he was arrested . . . he assembled us all, and said, "Before I am delivered to them, let us sing a hymn to the Father, and go to meet what lies before us." So he told us to form a circle, holding one another's hands, and he himself stood in the middle and said, "Answer *Amen* to me."

Then, as the disciples circled him, dancing, Jesus began to chant a hymn:

> "Glory to you, Father." And we, circling around him, answered him, "Amen."
> "Glory to you, Word [*logos*]; glory to you, Grace."
> "Amen."
> "We praise you, Father; we thank you, Light, in whom dwells no darkness."
> "Amen."

After the praises, Jesus continues this mystical chant as the others dance and chant in response to each phrase:

> "I will be saved, and I will save."
> "Amen."
> "I will be released, and I will release."
> "Amen."
> "I will wound, and will be wounded."
> "Amen."
> "I will eat, and I will be eaten."
> "Amen." . . .
>
> "I will play the flute. Dance, everyone."
> "Amen."

"I am a light to you who see me."
"Amen."
"I am a mirror to you who know me."
"Amen."

"I am a door to you who knock upon me."
"Amen."

As the dance progresses, Jesus invites those who dance to see themselves in him:

"You who follow my dance, see yourself in me, as I speak;
And if you have seen what I am doing, keep silent about my mysteries."

Through the dance and the singing, Jesus reveals the mystery of his passion: that he is going to suffer in order to show them their own suffering, so that they come to understand — and so transcend — it:

"You who dance, understand what I do; for yours is the human passion which I am to suffer. You could by no means understand what you suffer unless I had been sent to you by the Father, as the Word. You who have seen what I suffer, learn about suffering, and you will be able not to suffer."

As they dance and respond to his chant,

Jesus reveals that he suffers to teach a paradox much like what the Buddha also taught: that those who become aware of suffering and recognize it as universal simultaneously find release from it. Thus he invites them to join in the cosmic dance:

"Whoever dances belongs to the universe."
"Amen."
"Whoever does not dance does not know what happens."
"Amen."

Those who wrote down and revered the *Acts of John* apparently used this chant to celebrate the eucharist. But instead of eating bread and drinking wine "to proclaim the Lord's death" (*1 Corinthians* 11:26) as other Christians did, they chanted these words while holding hands and circling in the dance, celebrating together the mystery of Jesus's suffering and their own. Indeed, some Christians celebrate it like this to this day.

Thus the "good news" of the *Gospel of Judas* is that, as Paul wrote, "the sufferings of this present time are not worth comparing with the glory about to be revealed in us" (*Romans* 8:18). For although what happens to Jesus, so far as anyone in the world

144

can see, ends in the hideous anguish of crucifixion, and what happens to Judas ends in his murder, each has hope. Those who hear this message recognize that rather than being simply physical bodies with complex psychological components, we are fundamentally spiritual beings who need to discover what, in us, belongs to the spirit. This gospel suggests that our lives consist of more than what biology or psychology can explore — that our real life begins when the spirit of God transforms the soul.

The *Gospel of Judas,* then, seems to end in disaster: Jesus is betrayed; Judas will be stoned to death by his fellow disciples. But as we have seen, both have already achieved salvation. Jesus's sacrifice signals the end of death itself by acknowledging our fundamental spiritual nature. Gazing upward and entering into the luminous cloud, Judas is but the first-fruits of those who follow Jesus. His star leads the way.

A Final Note

"In order that human beings bring about the most radiant conditions for themselves to inhabit, it is essential that the vision of reality which poetry offers be transformative, more than just a printout of the given circumstances of its time and place."
— Seamus Heaney, "Joy or Night"

At the beginning of this essay on the *Gospel of Judas,* we asked what hope the author offers to redeem his anger. Have we found that hope, that vision? The *Gospel of Judas* is a hard text to read, not only because of its strange language of numbers and aeons, alien names, and breaks in the text but because of the strident anger that impels the author to mock and denounce those seeking meaning in the unjust execution and torture of friends and family. Sometimes his tone sounds cruelly offhand in its use of anti-Jewish and homophobic invective —

accusing presumably Jewish priests before the Temple of murder and same-sex relations, seemingly with no concern for how such throwaway lines of conventional polemic can harm people.

Yet in spite of his anger, *Judas*'s writer evokes a vision of "the most radiant conditions to inhabit" — a great and luminous temple of vibrant greenery in a place far from all the civilized evils of moral chaos and memory's oblivion — a glorious dream, especially for those who live in dry lands occupied and ruled by Roman legions. The measure of this gospel lies, as Heaney suggests, in its power to transform. Is there a transformative light in these pages? Not many early Christians, it would seem, found that here — except perhaps for those who copied this gospel and, as rumor has it, carefully preserved it in a limestone box, hidden away in a cave, guarded for centuries only by the dead. For the rest, the *Gospel of Judas* remained a path not taken, its horror of bodies tortured in God's name cast aside in favor of bright and unyielding stories of heroes who died for the faith.

We cannot understand this gospel — cannot read it as "good news" — apart from those circumstances of its time and place, apart from Roman persecution and the painful controversies it ignited. Recalling these things allows us to feel some empathy with this Christian, his grief, his anger, perhaps even his insistence on divine punishment as he imagines handing church leaders over to the path of death he feels they had chosen for themselves when they decided to worship a vengeful god. Like all moral texts, the *Gospel of Judas* might lead us to ask where we stand in our world of polarized religious violence. But that sympathy, and even that self-reflection, may not be enough; the luminous vision might be too shaded by anger and revenge to transform. Or perhaps not.

This long-hidden text now takes its place with such sources as the *Gospel of Thomas* and the *Gospel of Mary of Magdala.* The *Gospel of Judas,* far from being bizarre and marginal as we initially suspected, leads us right into the center of the debates about what Christianity would become. Like the other recently recovered texts, the *Gospel of Judas* helps give us a more detailed, complex, and above all more human account of the history of Christianity than anyone could have ever written without them. When we go on to place more familiar sources — the New Testament gospels and writings of the "church fathers" — in the context of their time and place, these recently discovered texts help us enormously. Within the New Testament gospels, too, we find alternating tones of fear and hope. Thus as one passage in the *Gospel of Judas* gives a negative picture of Jewish priests, so the New Testament gospels of *Matthew, Luke,* and *John* include passages sparked from ancient antagonisms that even now continue to incite hatred against Jews, contradicting whatever they say about love.[1] Historical investigation shows how these gospel traditions were generated out of intense conversations — traditions hotly contested, time and again, and often claimed by people who insist that they themselves are the only real Christians.

The recent discoveries help us see, too, how hard countless church leaders had to work to create the impression that many of us used to take for granted — that Christianity actually was a single, static, universal system of beliefs. Creating this impression was itself a remarkable achievement — one to which certain "fathers of the church" were dedicated. But they did so precisely because they realized how diverse Christian groups were, and they feared that controversies over basic issues — like those revealed in the *Gospel of Judas* — might undermine the "universal church" they were trying to build, along with the authority they were claiming for their church alone. Leaders like Irenaeus devoted decades of their lives to establishing the structures of creed, canon, clergy, believing that the movement's survival depended on them — and in some ways they may have been right, for there are limits to how many different views any group can accommodate, perhaps especially in times of trouble. But the recently discovered texts show us what was lost when they consolidated these institutions and silenced so many early Christian voices.

We ourselves investigate Christian traditions because we have found in them much to love, and much that speaks to our deepest convictions, fears, and hopes. When we find in the various gospels — both New Testament and non-canonical — elements that we cannot love, we are learning to own them as part of our history and to put them aside or engage them critically when it comes to faith and practice. In the process, we recognize that this is how Christians have dealt with the many traditions that make up Christianity for thousands of years. Each generation that engages them, and every group that does so, adopts, adapts, and transforms them just as we, and countless others, are doing today.

Many people have asked what we should do about these *other* gospels. Should we reopen the canon to include some of these long-rejected books? We think that doing so is not useful — and is beside the point. Church leaders established the canon at a specific and crucial time in history and for a specific purpose: to endorse a list of books "approved" for reading in public worship in order to unify the movement under their leadership. Certainly the canon has helped to do just that, since even today people who belong to an enormous range of churches — Methodist, Pentecostal, Baptist, Roman Catholic, Orthodox, Seventh Day Adventist, Episcopal, to name only a few — all draw upon the same collection of New Testament books, and read them in worship.

Gospels like this one, then, do not belong in the canon — nor, we think, do they belong in the trash. Instead, they belong where we have placed them here: within the history of Christianity. Yet it is because many of these texts also belong to the literature of spiritual transformation that they were written, read, copied, and loved by Christians over fifteen hundred years ago, and why they still intrigue many of us today. For even the writer of *Judas* moves beyond anger to revelation — when, for example, Jesus tells the disciples to "bring forth the perfect human," and reveals to Judas the brilliant realm of the spirit, illuminated by God's love. Exploring these discoveries, then, offers more than insight onto our past and present; it also opens up a far wider range of visions than we had ever imagined of what Jesus — and his teaching — might mean.

■ ■ ■ ■

PART TWO
THE GOSPEL OF JUDAS

■ ■ ■ ■

In the more than fifteen hundred years since the *Gospel of Judas* was inscribed in the Tchacos Codex, the text has suffered considerable damage. The worst came after its rediscovery in the 1970s, when improper handling and storage reduced much of it to tiny fragments. Despite the diligent work of an expert restoration team, it still contains many holes (called lacunae). Sometimes only a few letters are obscured, but some lacunae are quite extensive, leaving more than half a page empty. In the translation below, these are all marked with brackets: [. . .]; the number of ellipsis points within the brackets indicates approximately how many letters are missing. As much as possible, scholars have attempted to determine what was written in these lacunae, and these suggestions are also placed in brackets. In addition, I have supplied other material to render the translation into more fluid English prose or to suggest to readers the referents for some obscure pronouns; these materials are placed in parentheses: ().

This new translation is based on the Coptic text established by Rodolphe Kasser and Gregor Wurst[*]; all modifications of that text by myself or others are noted in the Comments section.

[*]*The Gospel of Judas. Coptic Text.* The National Geographic Society, April 2006 (published online at http://www.nationalgeographic.com/lostgospel/document.html), with modifications based on an advance copy of the critical edition of the Tchacos Codex edited by Rodolphe Kasser and Gregor Wurst; English translation by Marvin Meyer and F. Gaudard; notes by Marvin Meyer and Gregor Wurst, to be published by the National Geographic Society, Washington, D.C., spring 2007. We would like to thank Marvin Meyer for generously allowing us to see an advance copy of this edition. Any restorations proposed here, however, remain tentative until they can be confirmed by examination of the original manuscript of the announced facsimile edition.

English
Translation of the
Gospel of Judas
TRANSLATED BY KAREN L. KING

1[1] This is the hidden word of the pronouncement, [2]containing the account about wh[en Je]sus spoke with Judas [I]scari[ot] for eight days, three days before he observed Passover.

[3]When he appeared on earth, he performed signs and great wonders for the salvation of humanity. [4]For although some people continued to [walk] along the path of righteousness, [5]others were walking along the path of their transgression. [6]So twelve disciples were called, [7](and) he began to speak to them about the mysteries which are beyond the world and about the things which will occur at the end.

[8]Frequently, however, he would not reveal himself to his disciples, but you would find him in their midst as a child.

[9]And he dwelled in Judaea with his disciples.

2 **¹**One day he found them sitting, assembled together (and) training (themselves) in godliness. ²When he [came upon] his disciples assembled together, sitting and offering thanks over the bread, ³[he] laughed.

⁴The discipl[e]s said to him, "Teacher, why do you laugh at [our] offering thanks? Or what did we do? ⁵[This] is what is right."

⁶He replied, telling them, "It is not you I am laughing at — ⁷you are not even doing this by [yo]ur own will — ⁸but (I'm laughing because) in this (offering of thanks), your 'God' will receive praise."

⁹"Teacher, *you* are [. . . . .] the Son of our God," they said.

¹⁰Jesus said to them, "Do you (really think you) know me — how? ¹¹Truly I say to you, no race from the people among you will ever know me."

¹²Now when his disciples heard this, [they] began to be displeased and [become] angry, and to blaspheme against him in their heart.

¹³But when Jesus perceived their foolishness, ¹⁴[he said] to them, "Why are you letting anger disturb you? ¹⁵Your God who is within you and [his. . . .] are displeased [together with] your souls. ¹⁶Let whoever is [strong] among you humans bring forth the perfect human ¹⁷and stand up to face me."

[18]And they all said, "We are strong!" [19]But their spirits did not have the courage to stand up to face him — except Judas [Is]cariot. [20]He was able to stand up to face him, [21]even though he was not able to look him in the eyes, bu[t] turned his face aside.

[22]Judas said to him, "I know who you are and which place you came from — [23]you came from the realm of the immortal Barbelo — [24]but I am not worthy to proclaim the name of the one who sent you."

[25]Then Jesus, recognizing that he perceived even more of such exalted matters, said to him, "Separate from them. [26]I will tell you the mysteries of the kingdom. [27]It is possible for you to reach that place, [28]but you will suffer much grief. [29]For another [will] take your place, so that the twelve di[sciples] might again be complete in their 'God.' "

[30]And Judas said to him, "When will you tell these things to me, [31]and when will the great [da]y of the light dawn for the [. . . . . .] race?"

[32]But after he said these things, Jesus left him.

3 [1]When morning came, he [appear]ed to his disciples, [2][and] they said to him, "Teacher, where did you go? [3]What did you

do after you left us?"

⁴Jesus said to them, "I went to another great and holy race."

⁵His disciples said to him, "Lord, what great race is there that is more exalted and holier than we are, yet is not in these realms?"

⁶Now when Jesus heard these things, he laughed. ⁷He said to them, "What are you contemplating in your heart about the strong and holy race? ⁸[T]ruly [I] say to you that no offspring [of t]his realm will see that [race], ⁹nor will any angelic army of the stars rule over that race, ¹⁰nor will any mortal human offspring be able to belong to it. ¹¹For [t]hat rac[e] does not come from [this realm] which came into being [but. . . . . ¹²The r]ace of humans [who are] among [you (pl.)] is from the [r]ace of human[ity]. ¹³[. . . . .] power which [. . . . . . some ot]her for[ces. . . . . . .] since you rule i[n their midst]."

¹⁴When [his] disciples heard these things, each one of them was troubled i[n their] spirit, ¹⁵and they could not find a word to say.

4 ¹On another day, Jesus came up to [them]. ²They said to [him], "Teacher, we saw you in a [vision]. ³For we saw some great

dr[eam]s [at] night [. . .]

⁴[He said], "Why have [you. . . . . .] hid yourselv[es]?"

⁵For their part, they s[aid, "We] sa[w] a great hou[se in which there was a g]reat alta[r and] twelve men, whom we say are priests, and a name. ⁶But there was a crowd persevering tenaciously at that altar u[ntil] the priests [finish]ed [receiving] the offerings. ⁷As for us, we too [were] tenacious[ly per]severing.

⁸Je[sus said], "What ki[nd] of [priests are they]?

⁹They [said,] "[So]me [abstain for t]wo [w]eeks. ¹⁰Yet [others] sacrifice their own children, others their wives, ¹¹all the while praising and acting humbly toward each other. ¹²Some are lying with ma[l]es. ¹³Others work at slaughtering. ¹⁴Yet others were committing a [mul]titude of sins and injustices. ¹⁵[An]d the men who stand [ove]r the altar are invoking your na[me]! ¹⁶And so in all the labors of cutting up their sacrifices, that altar stays full." ¹⁷And when they had said these things, they were silent for they felt deeply disturbed.

¹⁸Jesus said to them, "Why are you disturbed? ¹⁹Truly I say to you, all the priests who stand ove[r that] altar are invoking my name. ²⁰And ag[ain] I say to you that they

wrote my name upon the [. . .] of the races of the stars through the races of human beings. ²¹[An]d in my name, they shamefully planted fruitless trees."

5¹Jesus said to them, "*You* are the ones you saw receiving offerings at the altar. ²That is the 'God' you serve. ³And you are the twelve men whom you saw. ⁴And the domestic animals you saw being brought for sacrifice are the multitude you are leading astray upon that al[t]ar. ⁵[The ruler of chaos will es]tablish himself, ⁶and this is how he will make use of my name. ⁷And the race of the pious will adhere tenaciously to him. ⁸After this, another man will take the side of the for[n]ic[ators], ⁹and another one will stand with those who murder children, ¹⁰and yet another with those who lie with men, ¹¹and those who fast, ¹²and all the rest of impurity and lawlessness and error,¹³ and those who say, 'We are equal to angels' — ¹⁴and they are the stars which bring everything to completion. ¹⁵For it has been said to the races of humans, 'Behold God received your sacrifice from the hands of a priest' — that is to say, from the minister of error. ¹⁶But it is the Lord — the one who is the Lord over the entire universe — who commands that they will be put to shame at the end of days."

17Jesus said [to them], "Cease sac[rificing. . . . .]. 18It is upon the alt[a]r that yo[u. . . . .] [for they are] over your stars and your angels, having already been completed there. 19Let them become [. . . .] again right in front of you, and let them . . .

6 [*about fifteen and a half lines are missing from the manuscript*]

to the races [. . .]. It is not possible for a bak[er] to feed the whole creation under [heaven]. And

[*about three and a half lines are untranslatable*]

71Jesus said to them, "Stop struggling against me. 2Each one of you has his own star a[nd every] o[ne . . .

[*about eighteen lines are missing from the manuscript or untranslatable*]

He came to those who [. . . . . . . sp]ring of the tree of [*about one line is untranslatable*] [sea]son of this realm [. . . . . af]ter a time [. . . . .]. Rather he came to water God's paradise and the [ra]ce that will endure, because [he wi]ll not pollute the way of [life of] that race. Bu[t. . . . .] for all eternity."

8 ¹Judas said to [him, "Rabb]i, What fruit does this race possess?"

²Jesus said, "The souls of every human race will die. ³But when those (who belong to the holy race) have completed the time of the kingdom and the spirit separates from them, ⁴their bodies will die but their souls will be alive and they will be lifted up."

⁵Judas said, "What, then, will the rest of the race of humans do?"

⁶Jesus said, "It is not possible to sow (seeds) upon a [s]ton[e] and have their [fr]uit be harvested. ⁷Again [thi]s is the way[. . . . .] the race [which is pol-lut]ed and perishable wisdom. ⁸[..] the hand which created mortal humanity so that their souls [g]o up to the realms which are on high. ⁹T[rul]y I say to you (pl.) th[at no ruler nor a]ngel [nor p]ower will be able to see [the places t]here, ¹⁰ which [this great] (and) holy race [will see]." ¹¹After Jesus said these things, he departed.

9 ¹Judas said, "Teacher, just as you listened to all of them, now listen to me also. ²For I have seen a great vision."

³But when Jesus heard, he laughed. ⁴He said to him, "Why are you getting all worked up, thirteenth god? ⁵But you too speak, and

I will hold you up."

6Judas said to him, "I saw myself in a vision. 7The twelve disciples were stoning me; 8they were persecuting [me severe]ly. 9And I [ca]me also to the place [. . . . .] after you. 10I saw [a house. . . . .] but my eyes were not able [to measure] its extent. 11But some elders of great stature were surrounding it, 12and that house was roofed with greenery. 13In the midst of the house wa[s a] cr[owd. . . . .]. 14Teacher, let me be taken [in wi]th these people."

15[Jesus] replied. He said, "Your star is leading you astray, Judas, 16since no mortal human offspring is worthy to enter the house that you saw. 17For that is the place which is preserved for the holy ones, 18the place where neither the sun nor the moon will rule them nor the day, 19but they will stand firm for all time in the realm with the holy angels. 20Behold, I have told you the mysteries of the kingdom 21and I have taught you [about the er]ror of the s[tar]s and [*about one and a half lines are untranslatable*] upon the t[w]elve realms."

22Judas said, "Teacher, surely the rulers are not subject to my seed?"

23Jesus answered. He said to him,

"Come . . . [24*about two lines are untranslatable*] 25[b]ut because you will groan deeply when you see the kingdom and its entire race."

26When Judas heard these things, he said to him, "What benefit have I received because you separated me for that race?"

27Jesus answered. He said, "You will become the thirteenth 28and you will be cursed by the rest of the races — 29but you will rule over them. 30In the last days, they will < > and you will go up to the holy ra[ce]."

10 1Jesus said, ["Com]e and I will [te]ach you about the [things. . . . . that] no human will see. 2For there exists a great realm and a boundlessness whose measure no angelic race has comprehended. 3[In] it is the great invis[ib]le Sp[irit] — 4the one whom no a[ngeli]c eye has seen nor any inner thought of heart contained nor has anyone called it by any name. 5And a luminous cloud appeared in that place.

6"And he said, 'Let an angel come into being to attend me.' 7And a great angel — the luminous divine Autogenes — came forth from the cloud. 8And another four angels came forth because of him from another cloud, 9and they came into being to attend the angelic Autogenes.

[10]"And [A]uto[genes] said, 'Let [Adamas] come into be[ing],' and [. . . . .] came into being. [11]And he c[reated] the first luminary so that [it] might rule over it. [12]Next he said, 'Let angels come into being to worship it,' [13]and immeasurable myriads came into being. [14]And he said, '[Le]t [a] luminous [re]alm come into being,' [15]and it came into being. [16]He established the second luminary to rule over it, [17]along with innumerable angelic myriads to worship (it). [18]And in this way, he created the rest of the realms of light, [19]he established (luminaries) to rule over them, [20]and he created for them innumerable angelic myriads for their service.

11 [1]"Adamas dwelled in the first cloud of the light, [2](yet) none among the angels — who are all called 'divine' — has seen that (cloud). [3]And he [*about two lines are untranslatable*] [4]the image [. . . . .] and according to the likeness of t[hat an]gel. [5]He made the imperishable [race] of Seth appear [. . . . .] the twelve [. . . . . .] the twenty [fo]ur [. . . . . .]. [6]By the will of the Spirit, he made seventy-two luminaries appear in the imperishable ra[ce]. [7]Then by the will of the Spirit, the seventy-two

luminaries themselves made three hundred sixty luminaries appear in the imperishable race in order that their number might become five for each.

8"And their father is the twelve realms of the twelve luminaries, 9with six heavens for every realm so that the seventy-two heavens might come into being for the seventy-two luminaries, 10with [five fi]rmaments for each one [of them so that] three hundred sixty [firmaments might come into being. . . . .]. 11They were given [an] authority with a [great, innumerab]le angelic army for glory and wor[ship], 12[and] then [in addition] virginal [sp]irits for gl[o]ry and [wor]ship of all the realms and the heavens and their [fi]rmaments.

12¹"Now it is that crowd of deathless ones who are called 'cosmos,' that is, 'what perishes.' ²It was by the Father and the seventy-two luminaries who are with Autogenes and his seventy-two realms that the first Human appeared in the place (the perishable cosmos) with his imperishable powers. ³For this realm, along with its race which appeared, is the one that has within it the cloud of knowledge and the angel who is called 'El.' ⁴[about 3 lines missing]

⁵"[Af]ter these things, he [. . . .] said, 'Let

168

the [tw]elve angels come into being [so they might r]ule over the chaos and the ob[livion].' [6]And behold an a[ngel] ap-[pear]ed from the cloud whose face was pouring forth fire, [7]while his likeness was defiled with blood. [8]And he had [one n]ame, 'Nebro,' which is interpreted as 'apostate,' [9]but some others call him 'I[al]dabaoth.' [10]And again another angel came forth from the cloud (called) 'Saklas.' [11]Nebro then created six angels along with Saklas to attend (him). [12]And these produced twelve angels in the heavens, [13]and each of them received an allotted portion in the heavens. [14]And the twelve rulers, along with the twelve angels said, 'Let each one of you . . .' [[15]*about three lines untranslatable*] [five] angels.

[16]"The first is [Se]th, who is called 'Christ.' [17]The [secon]d is Harmathoth, whom [. . . . .]. [18]The [thir]d is Falila. [19]The fo[u]rth is Iobel. [20]The fifth is Adonaios. [21]These are the five who ruled over oblivion and are first over chaos.

13[1]"Then Saklas said to his angels, 'Let us create a human being [ac]cording to the likeness and according to the image.' [2]Then they formed Adam and his wife, Eve. [3]But in the cloud, she was called 'Zoe' ('Life').

⁴For in this name all the races shall seek after it (life), ⁵and each one of them calls her by their names.

⁶"But [Sa]klas did not com[mand. . . . . . .] exce[pt. . . . .] the ra[ce]s [. . . . .] this one [. . . . .]. ⁷And the [ruler] said to him, 'Your life and that of your children will last (only) for a season.' "

⁸Judas said to Jesus, "[What] is the longest that a human being might live?"

⁹Jesus said, "Why are you surprised that the lifespan of Adam and his race is numbered in this place? ¹⁰It is in this place that he received his kingdom, with its ruler, for a (limited) number."

¹¹Judas said to Jesus, "Does the human spirit die?"

¹²Jesus said, "This is the way it is: God commanded Michael to loan the spirits of human beings to them so they might worship (him). ¹³Then the Great One commanded Gabriel to give the spirit with the soul to the spirits of the great undominated race. ¹⁴Because of this, the re[mai]ning souls will . . . [*about one and a half lines are untranslatable*] . . . light . . . [*about one and a half lines are untranslatable*] . . . ¹⁵to seek [after the] spirit within you (pl.) [which y]ou make to dwell in this [fle]sh among the races of the an[gel]s. ¹⁶Then God

required knowledge [to be given] to Adam and those with him [17]in order that the rulers of chaos and oblivion should not lord it over them."

14[1][Then] Judas said to Jesus, "What, then, will those races do?"

[2]Jesus said, "Truly I say to you (pl.), it is the stars that bring completion upon all things. [3]For when Saklas has completed his times which are fixed for him, [4]their first star will be about to come along with the races, [5]and those things which were spoken will be completed. [6]Then they will fornicate in my name, [7]and they will kill their children, [8]and . . .

[[9–10]*about eight and a half lines are untranslatable*]

. . . i]n my name, [11]and your star will r[ule] over the [thi]rteenth realm."

[12]But afterward, Jesus [lau]ghed.

[13][Judas sai]d, "Teacher, [why are you laughing at us?]"

[14][Jesus] re[pli]ed. [He said,] "It is not [yo]u (pl.) I am lau[gh]ing [at, bu]t at the error of the stars, [15]because these six stars go astray with these five warriors, [16]and all of them will be destroyed along with their creations."

[17]Then Judas said to Jesus, "What will

those who are baptized in your name do?"

¹⁸Jesus said, "Truly I say [to you], This baptism [. . . . .] my name . . .

[*about eight lines are untranslatable*]

. . . die [. . . . . . .] to me."

15¹"Truly [I sa]y to you, Judas, those [who of]fer up sacrifice to Sakla[s. . . . . g]od . . . [²*about three lines are untranslatable*] . . . everything [for they are w]icked. ³As for you, you will surpass them all. ⁴For you will sacrifice the human being who bears me. ⁵Already your horn is raised up, ⁶your anger is full, ⁷your star has passed by, ⁸and your heart has [preva]iled.

⁹"Tr[uly I say to you,] 'Your end . . .'

[¹⁰⁻¹¹ *about five and a half lines are untranslatable*]

. . . the ru[ler] who is destroyed. ¹²[An]d then the pl[a]ce of the great race of Adam will be exalted, ¹³because prior to heaven and earth and the angels, through the realms that race exists.

¹⁴"Behold, everything has been told to you. ¹⁵Lift up your eyes and see the cloud and the light which is in it and the stars which surround it. ¹⁶And the star that leads the way, that is your star."

¹⁷Then Judas lifted up his eyes. ¹⁸He saw the luminous cloud ¹⁹and he entered into

it. [20]Those standing upon the ground heard a voice coming from the cloud, saying, "[. . . . .] great ra[ce. . . . . im-]age . . ."

[*about six and a half lines are untranslatable*]

16[1][Then] their chief priests murmured because [he (Jesus)] entered [in]to the guest room for his prayer. [2]And some scribes were there watching closely in order to catch him at prayer, [3]for they were afraid of the people because he was held to be a prophet by them all.

[4]And they approached Judas. [5]They said to him, "What are you doing in this place? [6]You are the disciple of Jesus."

[7]But as for him, he answered them according to their will. [8]Then Judas received some copper coins. [9]He handed him over to them.

[10]The Gospel of Judas

COMMENTS ON THE TRANSLATION

1:1 The first word in the *Gospel of Judas* is *logos,* which means "word," "speech," or "account." For readers of the *Gospel of John,* the Word (*logos*) is Jesus ("In the beginning was the Word. . . . And the Word became flesh and lived among us. . . . No one has ever seen God. It is God the only Son, who is close to the Father's heart, who has made him known"; *John* 1:1, 14, 18). The author of the *Gospel of Judas* very likely was acquainted with the *Gospel of John* and may be referring to it in this way. As in the *Gospel of John,* in *Judas* it is Jesus who reveals the unknown (hidden) nature of God.

This kind of double meaning also occurs with the term translated here as "pronouncement" (*apophasis*), which has two connotations: "something declared openly" and "a court judgment." Jesus's teaching has both of these meanings in the *Gospel of*

Judas: He speaks plainly to Judas, but his words also serve as a kind of judgment against the other disciples. Again, this is very similar to the *Gospel of John,* which presents Jesus as the revelation of God in the world; he saves some with his teaching but shows that others are condemned: "God did not send the Son into the world to condemn the world, but in order that the world might be saved through him. Those who believe in him are not condemned; but those who do not believe are condemned already . . ." (*John* 3:17–18). In both gospels, Jesus comes to bring salvation, but the disciples are judged based on whether or not they understand who Jesus is and where he comes from.

Interesting as well, "pronouncement" (*apophasis*) is also the title of an earlier writing that the third-century church father Hippolytus (*Heresies* 6:11) attributes to the (in)famous heretic Simon the Magician, who is mentioned in *Acts* 8:9–24. The *Gospel of Judas* is clearly not this spurious work, but the similarity in title might raise the question about whether the author of the *Gospel of Judas* wants to relate his gospel to other streams of second-century Christianity.

1:2 The odd calculation of the period during which the events described in the *Gospel of Judas* take place seems to indicate that the conversations with Judas extended over a week (eight days) and ended three days before the Passover when Jesus was put to death.

1:3 The *Gospel of Judas* does not tell about Jesus's "birth" (like infancy narratives in *Matthew* and *Luke*) or about his "becoming flesh" (like the prologue to the *Gospel of John*), but instead it talks about his "appearance" or "revelation." This terminology indicates that he is divine, but it leaves the question of incarnation in the flesh unclear.

Jesus's miracles demonstrate both his divinity and his purpose in coming, and at the same time contrast God's true nature with that of the world rulers. The *Gospel of Judas* begins by saying that Jesus's purpose was to save humanity, in part by performing miracles that recall what Christians already knew — how he healed the sick and ailing, and cared for those who were hungry, needy, and demon-possessed. The New Testament gospels, and many others as well, also speak of Jesus's miracles in order to show his divine nature. The *Gospel of John,* for example, ends by saying: "Jesus did many other signs in the presence of his disciples, which are not written in this book.

But these are written so that you may come to believe that Jesus is the Messiah the Son of God, and that through believing you may have life in his name" (*John* 20:30–31). All the New Testament gospels tell how Jesus performed miracles; in the *Gospel of Judas,* as in the *Testimony of Truth,* these healings not only demonstrate God's compassion but also show that illness and death are evils inflicted by the lesser powers that rule the world — not by God. Thus the *Gospel of Judas* shows that when Jesus heals those who suffer, he demonstrates that God wills human salvation — life and wholeness.

1:4–5 Here we see what motivated God to send Jesus: Not everyone was righteous. Jews and Christians commonly described salvation as turning away from "transgressions" to righteousness as the *Gospel of Judas* does here, but it also emphasizes that not all who think they are already righteous really are righteous. Throughout the gospel, Jesus will introduce themes that, like this one, are common to Jewish and Christian stories of the end time: anger, judgment, and the collapse of moral and cosmic order.

1:6 The New Testament gospels all say that Jesus called disciples at the beginning of his ministry, and at the end of three of those (*Matthew, Luke,* and *John*), they are sent out to preach the gospel. Here, however, the disciples are not commissioned to go out and preach the gospel; instead, it illustrates how "some walk along the path of righteousness, others were walking along the path of their transgression." Originally, Judas belongs to "the twelve"; only later will he be "separated" from them by Jesus, and then killed by the other disciples. Judas himself will be replaced by another disciple, so that the number of "the twelve" is maintained. This number is symbolic, linking the twelve disciples with the twelve rulers of the lower world. What is shocking here is what the *Gospel of Judas* implies: that only those who misunderstood and rejected Jesus's teaching were left to carry on after his death. The only hope of rectifying this situation lies in the secret account of Jesus's teaching from the *Gospel of Judas* itself!

1:7 Here the author introduces the two main themes of Jesus's secret teaching to Judas: the nature of the divine world above and the end of the world.

1:8 This sentence seems to interrupt the flow of the story in the way that it directly addresses the reader ("you"), and may have been added later; for even though the *Gospel of Judas* was originally written (in Greek) in the second century, the only copy that exists comes from the fourth century (in Coptic translation). We can safely assume that copyists felt free to alter (i.e., "improve") the text during the centuries in which it was passed on — a very common practice even with regard to the New Testament.[1] But why would they have thought that adding this sentence was an improvement? It indicates that the disciples were not able to perceive who Jesus was when he appeared "as a child" — yet another indication of their lack of spiritual insight.

The idea that Jesus sometimes took the form of a child may seem unusual to modern audiences as well, but it appears in many ancient texts. Two of the New Testament gospels, the *Matthew* and *Luke,* tell of Jesus's birth, and *Luke* also has a story of Jesus as a young man impressing the elders in the Temple with his wisdom (*Luke* 2:41–52). This picture of Jesus as a wise child is elaborated in greater detail in the legendary second-century *Infancy Gospel of Thomas,* in which Jesus confounds his poor teacher, Zacchaeus, and curses some children who wrong him by striking them dead. Although Jesus raises the children back to life in the end, he laughs at how the adults misunderstand his actions, admonishing them to greater insight: "Now let that which is yours

179

bear fruit, and let the blind in heart see. I have come from above to curse them and call them to the things above, as He commanded who sent me for your sakes" (*Infancy Gospel of Thomas* 8:1). This portrait of Jesus laughing is very reminiscent of Jesus in the *Gospel of Judas,* when he laughs at the foolishness of his disciples and admonishes them to higher spiritual vision. In the *Gospel of Thomas,* it is Jesus himself who teaches about the wisdom to be learned from children. He tells his disciples that "the person old in days won't hesitate to ask a little child seven days old about the place of life, and that person will live" (*Gospel of Thomas* 4), but the point is not so much about Jesus as a child but that creation (the pristine universe God created in seven days, represented here by a seven-day-old child) holds the whole meaning of life. So, too, in the *Gospel of Matthew,* Jesus tells his disciples that they must "change and become like children" in order to enter the kingdom of heaven (*Matthew* 18:1–6; 19:13–15). In the *Secret Revelation of John,* Christ appears in many brilliant forms to the apostle John, first as a young man and then as an elder, in order to show John that he did not abandon him, but that for those who are perceptive, he appears in many forms (*SRJ* 3:4–13). In the *Gospel of the Savior,* Jesus explicitly tells his disciples, "I am in your midst as the little children" (*Gospel of the Savior* 107:57–60), and later tradition will also picture the Spirit who guides Paul as a child (*Apocalypse of Paul* 18:3–22). In all of these cases, including the *Gospel of Judas,* the image of the child points to the hidden or unexpected presence of the divine.

Jesus's appearance as a child also shows that the physical body is not a limitation for the spirit; rather, it demonstrates how malleable the body is. Its birth, growth, and death are only appearances compared with the eternal stability of the spirit.

2:1 The term here is *gymnaze,* which means to "exercise" or "train," and is related to the English terms "gymnasium" and "gymnastic." It refers to doing something or acting a particular way in order to gain proficiency at something. Here the disciples are gaining proficiency in ⲘⲚⲦⲚⲞⲨⲦⲈ, literally "divinity" or "reverence toward God." In other words, they are performing certain actions — here offering thanks over the bread — in order to cultivate a pious character and true devotion. This idea belongs to the ancient belief that doing certain acts helps to cultivate corresponding inner attitudes; so, for example, if one acts generously toward others, one actually comes to feel generous, or if one wears a veil, one will develop a modest attitude.

2:2 The term here is *eucharisti,* which literally means "to give thanks," but by the second century, when the *Gospel of Judas* was written, it was becoming a technical term for the Christian celebration of the eucharist, the meal in which Christians communally eat bread as the body of Christ in memory of his death.

2:3–9 Whenever Jesus laughs in the *Gospel of Judas,* he is about to correct errors in someone's thinking. In this instance, Jesus's laughter is a kind of ridicule or mockery intended to shock the disciples out of their complacency and false pride. Their deepest problem is that they don't know they have a problem; they wrongly think they are already righteous, with their prayers and practices of piety. Jesus tries to teach them that they are not worshipping the true God. At first they are astonished, not understanding, and they insist (wrongly) that Jesus is the Son of "our" God. The very fact that they are celebrating the eucharist shows that they are wrong in their understanding that God demands Jesus's death as a sacrifice. The author of the *Gospel of Judas* is reading the situation of his own day back into the gospel story, since Christians did not celebrate the eucharist as a sacrificial meal until after Jesus's death. But the author's point here is that Jesus himself opposed this (later) practice, because it misconstrued the true meaning of his death, as the author sees it.

2:10 Coptic has two words for "know" or "knowledge." One of them refers to cognitive understanding (ⲉⲓⲙⲉ); the other, to intimate acquaintance or personal experience (ⲥⲟⲟⲩⲛ). Jesus uses the second term here, which could also be translated as "Do you recognize me?" The point is that the disciples think they understand who Jesus is, but in fact they don't really know him at all — and as long as they don't recognize their ignorance, they will never come to know him.

2:11 When Jesus declares that none of his disciples ("no race from the people among you") will ever know him, he is saying that people who consider themselves to be "children" of the false "God" will never be able to perceive who Jesus is — that he is the Son of the true God above.

The term the author uses here is *genos,* which could be translated "kind," "people," or "race." Contrary to the notion that Christians broke down barriers of race, class, and gender (as in *Galatians* 3:28, "There is no longer Jew or Greek, there is no longer slave or free, there is no longer male or female; for all of you are one in Christ Jesus"), they continued to use the language of ethnic and racial identity to understand Christians as a people, often calling themselves "a third race."[2] This language of "race" appears frequently in the *Gospel of Judas.* Although the author often uses the plural "human races," in essence only two races exist: the mortal race (those who worship the false Gods of the lower world and are destined to be destroyed at the end of the age) and the immortal race (those who recognize their own spiritual nature and turn to the true God above).

A similar idea is stated clearly in another book from Nag Hammadi, the *Sophia of Jesus Christ,* in which Jesus teaches that "(e)verything that came from the perishable will perish, since it came from the perishable. But whatever came from imperishableness does not perish but becomes imperishable. So, many people went astray because they had not known this difference and they died" (III.98:1–9). Death, it would seem, is not inevitable, but a result of not learning how to distinguish between the mortal world where people live now and the eternal world above. Since humanity is created in the image of the divine Adamas above — in that sense, people come from the imperishable — they are capable of becoming imperishable.

2:12 Instead of accepting Jesus's teaching and repenting, asking for further instruction, or changing their ways, the disciples become angry and commit blasphemy. Their reaction may be an indication of how some Christians responded when the author of the *Gospel of Judas* confronted his fellow Christians with what he regarded as their erroneous understanding of Jesus's death.

2:13–15 Jesus, being divine, of course knows what the disciples are thinking. The author uses the term ⲙⲛⲧⲁⲧϩⲏⲧ, which means "the state of being without heart/mind"; in other words, the disciples are described as witless and foolish, lacking in sound judgment and understanding. Jesus tells them that the anger that disturbs them comes from "the God within" — not the true God above, but the lower God whom they worship. This passage is extremely important, as it indicates one of the core assumptions the author is making: that people come to be like the God they worship. If people worship the true God, they strengthen the divine Spirit within so that their souls are shaped for eternal life, but if they worship the Gods of the lower material world, they become like them — angry, self-righteous, ignorant, and violent.

The altercation between Jesus and his disciples over their eucharist practice is strongly reminiscent of *John* 6:35–64, where Jesus disputes with his disciples over where Jesus comes from and what it means to say that Jesus's flesh is the true bread of life. There, Jesus teaches that "unless you eat the flesh of the Son of Man and drink his blood, you have no life in you. Those who eat my flesh and drink my blood have eternal life, and I will raise them up on the last day; for my flesh is true food and my blood is true drink" (*John* 6:53–55). His followers murmur against him, and he rebukes them, "Does this offend you? Then what if you were to see the Son of Man ascending where he was before? It is the spirit that gives life; the flesh is useless. The words that I have spoken to you are spirit and life" (*John* 6:61–63). The author of the *Gospel of John* writes that many followers of Jesus were offended and left him because of this hard saying, but "the twelve" remained faithful — while Judas is named for the first time as the betrayer.

The *Gospel of Judas* reverses this scene,

186

at least in part, for those disciples who truly understand, like Judas, are the ones who reject the idea that Jesus's flesh brings salvation. For the author of the *Gospel of Judas,* they are the ones who rightly understand Jesus's teaching in the *Gospel of John* that "the flesh is useless." Jesus will be crucified, but it is his ascent to heaven — and the ascent of those he draws with him — that is the true meaning of salvation. Do we have here, then, a portrait of the later situation — that some of Jesus's followers rejected the implied cannibalism of the sacrifice meal and that Judas, the betrayer, was among them? Or might it only be that the author of the *Gospel of Judas,* reading the *Gospel of John,* identified Judas with Christians in his own day who rejected Jesus's death as a sacrifice? We can only speculate, but in either case, this passage from the *Gospel of John* may help us understand better why some Christians thought that Judas was the one disciple who understood Jesus's teaching.

2:16–17 Note here how Jesus calls the disciples "you humans" but then demands they show forth "the perfect human." The pun is that they don't know what it means to be really human. They don't understand, as Judas will learn, that their true nature is not mortal flesh; rather the lower gods created all humanity in the divine image of "the perfect human" — the heavenly Adamas above — following the author's interpretation of *Genesis* 1:26–27.

2:18–21 Here again the disciples show their arrogance and their ignorance, for when Jesus tells them to stand before him, they are at first bold, claiming, "We are strong!" but then they are unable to face up to him. Only Judas manages to find the courage.

The irony is that even though the disciples are trying to train themselves to be pious, in fact they are easily angered, quickly led to blasphemy, and cowardly. In portraying them like this, the *Gospel of Judas*'s author purposefully invokes a widespread belief that a person's spiritual character is demonstrated by mental and emotional stability ("standing firm") or their lack. Michael A. Williams[3] has studied this theme extensively and come to two conclusions that are important here. First, Greek philosophers following Plato distinguished a perfectly stable, immovable, and unchanging divine realm from the changeable and unstable world of material things. So too Jesus is going to teach Judas that there is an unshakable divine world beyond this one. Second, people's behavior is shaped by whether they follow the pattern of the higher divine stability or the lower agitation of material things. Williams gives a good example from the first-century Jewish philosopher Philo of Alexandria, who argues that "(t)he foolish person's nature is to be moving constantly contrary to right reason, to be hostile to stillness and rest, and never to stand firmly. The soul of the worthless person is 'constantly shaken' since it has no firm footing. . . . By contrast, the wise man has stilled the swell and tossing of the soul. . . . His actions are not . . . easily shaken." The best example is Abraham, who stood steadfastly before God. In the *Gospel of Judas,* when the disciples are unable to stand up to Jesus, it is clear that they lack the spiritual calm that comes from stability of character and closeness to God. Judas is depicted as superior to them because he can stand before Jesus, but even he has to avert his eyes, showing that he has not yet arrived at the highest spiritual state. He eventually does achieve this in the end, when Jesus instructs Judas to "lift up his eyes." When Judas obeys, he ascends to the unchanging spiritual realm — the luminous cloud above.

2:22–24 Here we get the first indication of why Jesus promotes Judas over the others. He alone recognizes who Jesus really is: "I know who you are and which place you came from." In the New Testament gospels as well, the disciples struggle and often fail to understand Jesus's true identity. For example, in the *Gospel of Mark,*[4] only Peter understands that Jesus is the Christ; but even he rejects Jesus's crucifixion, and Jesus turns on him, calling him Satan and charging, "You are setting your mind not on divine things but on human things" (*Mark* 8:27–33).[5] Jesus's disciples in the *Gospel of John* also fail to recognize Jesus; even though they claim they have understood, at the end, they all desert him — and Peter actually denies him three times (*John* 14:1–11; 16:28–32; 18:15–27).[6] Like the disciples in the *Gospel of John,* who flee at Jesus's arrest, the disciples in the *Gospel of Judas* are afraid: proof that they do not really believe, because they do not really understand who Jesus is and where he comes from.

The term translated "realm" here is *aeon,* which means "a period of time," "an age," "a lifetime." In adverbial form, *aionios,* it means "eternity." The term appears frequently in the *Gospel of Judas* to refer both to the immortal, eternal realm above and to the mortal, limited realm below. It thus has a very strong spatial as well as temporal connotation. In other Christian texts, the term is also sometimes personified, so that it refers to a kind of eternal being — like angels or archangels — but here the main sense is a realm that exists with regard to a period of time (whether limited or eternal).

The name Barbelo will be unfamiliar to most readers, and indeed she appears only once in the *Gospel of Judas,* but this figure is familiar from other ancient texts discovered in Egypt over the last century. Many of these belong to a type of Christianity scholars call Sethianism (or Sethian Gnosticism), because these works claim that the spiritual race of humanity is descended from Adam's third son, Seth (or Eve's daughter, Norea). In these works, Barbelo appears as the divine Mother, the second figure of the Divine triad: Father (the Invisible Spirit), Mother (Barbelo), Son (Autogenes, the Self-generated One, Christ). In many such works, the "realm of Barbelo" encompasses the whole divine sphere above, so it is a kind of short-hand reference to the divine realm.[7]

2:25–32 When Jesus hears Judas, he recognizes that he has spiritual insight and is capable of learning more and so will be able to go up to the place where Jesus comes from. Jesus promises to teach him more about "the mysteries of the kingdom," which, we later learn, concern the origin and nature of the universe.

He also tells Judas to separate himself from the others, perhaps a practice also encouraged by the author of the *Gospel of Judas* and a strong indication that this group is on the defensive and has drawn away from other Christians, who hold different views about sacrifice and martyrdom. Here Jesus tells Judas for the first time that he will suffer a great deal at the hands of the other disciples, again perhaps an indication of how strained the relations are among Christians in the author's day. The author presupposes that Judas was at first one of "the twelve" but was later replaced when Jesus separated him for special teaching and a special assignment — to hand him over. The New Testament *Acts of the Apostles* 1:15–26 also tells a story in which the disciples replace Judas with another disciple, Matthias.

But why does Judas need to be replaced at all? The author says it is in order that "the twelve" may be "complete in their 'God.' " Here for the first time we see an emphasis on the meaning of numbers, which is even more pronounced later when Jesus teaches Judas about the origin of the world. As will later become clear, the significance of the number twelve is that the true God set twelve angels to rule over the lower world; the twelve disciples thus represent on earth the number of "their 'God' " in heaven.

We see something similar in one of the other texts inscribed in the Tchacos Codex, the *First Apocalypse of James,* also known from a copy found near Nag Hammadi in 1945. In the Nag Hammadi version, again we see one disciple elevated above the rest; here it is James. Jesus sends him to "rebuke the Twelve" because they are mired in false contentment, wrongly thinking that they have "the way of knowledge" (*1 Apocalypse of James* NH 42:20–24), just as we see Jesus condemning "the twelve" for their false piety in the *Gospel of Judas.* But this text elevates a set of other disciples in their stead: Jesus praises seven of his women disciples and instructs James to be "persuaded by [the testimony] of Salome and Mariam [and Martha and Ars]inoe."[8] The version in the Tchacos Codex offers a somewhat different reading (any specific rebuke addressed to "the twelve" is probably contained in a lost portion of the text, at 29:12–19), but the praise of the women is considerably sharper. This version calls the seven women disciples "the seven spirits" and names them: wisdom, insight, counsel, strength, understanding, knowledge, and fear (of God) (26:4–10). Six human women are mentioned by name as models of salvation: Salome, Mary, Arsinoe, Sapphira, Susanna, and Joanna.[9]

3:1–13 When Jesus left his disciples, he ascended "to another great and holy race." Readers learn here that Jesus is by no means trapped in "the prison of his body" and needing to be saved from it, as some church fathers from the second century claimed heretics believed. Instead, he is easily able to move between this world and the world above.

The disciples are surprised to learn that there is a race living in realms beyond this world. Their ignorance and disbelief again cause Jesus to laugh — signaling the reader that important teaching is to follow. Here Jesus distinguishes clearly between the mortal children of the lower world and the race that comes from the realm above. The race from above is strong and holy, and is not subject to the angels or stars that govern the lower world — a point Jesus will stress again (see also 9:17–19). In contrast, people who worship the lower angels are thereby enslaved to them, reminding one of Paul's teaching in *Galatians* 4:8–11: "Formerly, when you did not know God, you were enslaved to beings that by nature are not gods. Now, however, that you have come to know God, or rather to be known by God, how can you turn back again to the weak and beggarly elemental spirits? whose slaves you want to be once more? How can you want to be enslaved again? You are observing special days, and months, and seasons, and years. I am afraid that my work for you may have been wasted." Here Paul upbraids Christians in the Galatian churches for following the ritual calendar, seeing it as enslavement to the elemental spirits, which are associated with the heavenly bodies that set the calendar. Similarly, the *Book of Revelation* pictures pure believers living eternally in the New Jerusalem, where they will "need no light of lamp or sun, for the Lord God will be their light" (*Revelation* 22:5).

Again the twelve disciples' reaction shows that they don't really understand, for Jesus's teaching upsets them and they don't even know how to ask Jesus to clarify what he is saying.

4:1–7 The *Gospel of Judas* contains accounts of two dreams, the first by the twelve disciples, the second by Judas. Both come to Jesus to help them understand the meaning of what they have seen, and in both cases Jesus uses the dreams to correct the false beliefs and practices of his disciples. The dream of "the twelve," however, stands in contrast to the dream Judas will have, for while "the twelve" see only the violence and immorality of life in this world, Judas grasps a partial vision of the realm above.

In their dream the twelve disciples see "a great house." This is a temple (a house of God) before which sacrifices are offered, most likely understood to be the Jewish Temple in Jerusalem. Twelve priests stand before the altar, receiving offerings from a crowd. They also perceive "a name." The disciples see themselves in the dream among the crowd, devoted to the altar.

4:8–21 Jesus directs the disciples' attention more closely to the priests (or "the crowd"? — a reading would fit in the lacunae as well as "the priests," but the meaning is not clear, since it is the job of priests to sacrifice, although it is plausible that the author wants us to think that the crowd adopts the immoral behavior of its leaders). The disciples then tell him more about what they are doing. It is shocking: They are sacrificing their own wives and children, engaging in illicit sex, slaughter, and "a multitude of sins and injustices." And yet the altars stay full! Readers also learn here that "the name" the priests are invoking is that of Jesus.

Again the disciples are upset and silent. Jesus condemns the priests, because they are using his name shamefully to plant "fruitless trees" — a charge closely resembling those that other Christians aimed at one another. In the New Testament book of *2 Peter,* for example, the author charges other Christians as "false prophets" and "false teachers," who "indulge their flesh in depraved lust" and entice others into "licentious desires"; they are "slaves of corruption," "like irrational animals," "waterless springs," and so on. The author assures his readers that they will all be condemned and punished (*2 Peter* 2:1–22). The charges of murder and same-sex relations, too, belong to the general theme in ancient thought that impiety leads to violence and sexual immorality (see, for example, *Romans* 1:18–32).[10] The *Apocalypse of Peter* also calls those Christians who are praising Jesus for his death on the cross "blind and deaf" (73:13–14) — showing yet again that charges of error and immorality were flying in all directions.

5:1–19 Now Jesus gives them the full interpretation of the dream, equating "the twelve" with the priests at the altar and the offerings with people that they lead astray. All the immoral acts and violence they witnessed in the dream result from worshipping the lower "God," who uses Jesus's name to set himself up falsely as the true God. It is this lower "God" who demands sacrifices, but he is merely a "minister of error" (5:15). Jesus calls upon his disciples to stop this behavior, to quit sacrificing themselves and others to this false "God" who said that at the resurrection they will "be like angels" — even as the *Gospel of Luke* said that Jesus taught that "those who are considered worthy of a place in that age and in the resurrection from the dead . . . cannot die anymore, because they are like angels (literally "equal to angels") and are children of God" (*Luke* 20:35–36). Here Jesus teaches that if people do not stop this behavior, at the end of days the true Lord of the universe will put them all to shame. The mention of the "end of days" is yet another instance where the author draws upon apocalyptic imagery and belief in God's final condemnation of the unrighteous. This will happen when the stars complete everything — a reference to Jesus's teaching about the heavenly sphere, which will become more clear later.

In 5:7, Jesus says that the pious will adhere to something. But what? Grammatically, the referent is ambiguous. It could mean that the so-called pious will adhere to the ruler of chaos or it could mean that they will adhere to Jesus's name. In either case, it is clear that the world ruler leads people astray through Jesus's name.

6–7 These pages are heavily damaged, so we have to speculate about what is being conveyed. One clear point of interest is Jesus's insistence that everyone has a star — again referring to teaching about the heavenly bodies that Jesus will clarify later in his revelation to Judas.

The end of chapter 7 seems to contain an interpretation of the garden paradise described in *Genesis.* It refers to the springs that water it and to a tree. Someone (Christ) provides "water" (knowledge?) to the "race that will endure" (the children of Seth?) so that they will not be polluted. It may be an amplification of what Jesus means when he later tells Judas that God gave knowledge to Adam and those with him so that they could escape the domination of the lower-world rulers (see *Judas* 13:16–17).

8:1–8 Judas asks about Jesus's interpretation of the "fruit" — presumably the fruit of the tree of knowledge or the tree of life, from the *Genesis* story of the trees of paradise, which Jesus had been discussing in chapter 7. In response to his question, Jesus again talks about the two races. All the souls of people who belong to the mortal race will die when their bodies perish and the divine Spirit leaves them. But those who belong to the immortal race will have a different fate: When their bodies perish, the Spirit will lift up their souls to eternal life. Judas can't seem to understand what Jesus is saying, because he asks again about what happens to those who don't ascend at death. Although Jesus's response is in a section of severely damaged manuscript, he seems to answer Judas that it is possible for them to ascend as well. Jesus refers first to the parable of the sower (e.g., *Matthew* 13:1–23; *Mark* 4:1–20; *Luke* 8:4–15; *Thomas* 9), indicating that those who are polluted with the wisdom of the world (see also *Judas* 10:4) are like seeds falling on stone: Nothing can be harvested from them. But then he speaks about a "hand" that created human beings so that they *can* ascend to the heavenly realm.

It would appear that the fate of one's soul depends upon whether one turns inward to discover the Spirit within or whether one lives according to the standards of the world ("corruptible wisdom"), notions common in the second century. Plato had already argued something similar in the *Phaedo,* in which Socrates, about to be put to death by poisoning, discusses with friends the fate of the soul. He argues that when the soul is in bondage to the body, pains and pleasures are like nails that rivet the soul to the body and make the soul "corporeal." The result is that the soul then "fancies the things are true which the body says are true. For because it has the same beliefs and pleasures as the body, it is compelled to adopt also the same habits and mode of life, and can never depart in purity to the other world, but must always go away contaminated with the body. . . . Therefore it has no part in communion with the divine and pure and absolute." In contrast, those who cultivate the virtuous life of the soul have no fear at the death of the body, knowing that death will only free the soul for immortal life with the divine. Those with a prophetic spirit, Socrates claims, go to their deaths with joy, because "they are to go to the god whose servants they are."[11] In the *Gospel of Judas,* too, this fate belongs to the one disciple who has a prophetic spirit capable of receiving divine revelation: Judas. We can assume that all those who accepted the teaching of the

Gospel of Judas also thought that they, too, were on the spiritual path to God.

9:1–5 Now Judas has a great vision and asks Jesus to listen to him as well as to "the twelve." Jesus responds to his request by laughing, again leading us to ask what is wrong with Judas's request. Judas is "all worked up" — showing a kind of instability of character readers have come to associate with "the twelve" — but Jesus offers to "hold (him) up." The metaphor indicates that Jesus's teaching supports Judas, helping him to stand firm and gain the stability he needs in order to develop spiritually.

Jesus here calls Judas "thirteenth god." The word translated "god" here is *daimon,* which Christians will later understand as a negative entity ("demon"). In Greek thought, however, the term *daimon* was used to indicate gods of a lower rank, or sometimes an individual's lot or fortune. Indeed, Plato wrote that everyone possesses a *daimon:*

As regards the most lordly kind of soul found in us, we must conceive of it like this: we declare that God has given to each of us as a *daimon* that kind of soul which is housed in the top of our body and which raises us up from the earth towards our kindred [*suggeneian*] in heaven, seeing that we are not an earthly plant but a heavenly one.[12]

By devoting one's life to cultivating this *daimon,* one can achieve likeness to God and immortality, which is one's supreme happiness (*eudaimonia* — literally, the state of a good *daimon*). If, on the other hand, a person cultivates the lower parts of the soul, which are devoted to mortal things like wealth and appetite, then that person truly becomes mortal.

The number thirteen is also significant. It signals that Judas is beyond or outside the group of "the twelve." Moreover, as noted above (*Judas* 2:29), the number twelve belongs to the rulers of the lower world, whom the twelve disciples worship. Thus the number thirteen also expresses that Judas has surpassed the twelve rulers of the world, implying that he is no longer under the dominion of the twelve rulers of the lower world.

9:6–14 When Judas tells Jesus about his dream, the reader understands why he is upset: He sees himself being stoned and persecuted by the twelve disciples. Like other Christians in the author's day who face the possibility of suffering and martyrdom, Judas is afraid.

But his vision does not end there. He sees himself ascending to the heavenly realm, probably following "after [Jesus]." There Judas sees a great house. In contrast to the dream of "the twelve," he sees not an earthly building but the heavenly temple of the true God above.[13] No priests are offering sacrifices there; instead, it is described as a place of greenery surrounded by wise elders (ϩⲛⲛⲟϭ ⲛⲣⲱⲙⲉ, literally "some large, great, or old people"). This language is used as a title of respect for an elder, especially a person of notable stature (like the Christian use of "presbyter"). It is reminiscent, too, of the biblical figure of God as "Ancient One" in *Daniel* 7:9, 13, 22; and the image of God reigning and manifesting his glory "before his elders" (*Isaiah* 24:23). Here the elders appear to be distinguished members of the divine court standing before the heavenly temple of God. This temple, too, is filled with a crowd (presumably the great and holy race?), and Judas asks Jesus to let him join them.

Not only the contrast but also the *similarity* between the two dreams (the two temples, the two groups who lead, and the two crowds who worship at each) is deliberate, for this likeness points to the way in which everything in this world is but an inferior and misleading imitation of the true reality in the divine realm above, as Jesus will reveal to Judas, beginning in chapter 10.

9:15–21 We now learn what it is that Judas has misunderstood: He apparently thought that members of the mortal human race could enter the heavenly temple. But Jesus corrects this mistake, saying that it is reserved for the holy ones. Here all those who have escaped the dominion of the heavenly bodies — the sun, the moon, and the day — will live forever with the holy angels. Judas had apparently thought that after suffering death his body would be resurrected. Such is the "teaching" of the errant heavenly bodies — the stars (planets) of the lower world. But Jesus's teaching lets him know that death is nothing to fear.

9:22–25 At last Judas begins to understand Jesus's deeper message. He is astonished to realize that "(his) seed" — that is, all those who belong to the holy immortal race — is superior to the lower angels who rule the world. Since Judas and those like him possess the immortal divine spirit while the angelic rulers exist only for an allotted time, the seeming order of things is reversed: It is the lower angels who are in fact subject to the immortal race. This view is reminiscent of *Hebrews* 1–2, which stresses that Christ is superior to the angels, citing a "revisionist" Christianized version of Psalm 8 (which declares that "man" was made "little less than God").

Judas's realization is balanced, however, with yet another prophecy that he will "groan deeply" over his role in this world, for his understanding of the truth about the kingdom of this world and the mortal human race will lead him to grieve over their fate.

9:26–30 Now Judas begins to wonder if it is all worth it, but Jesus comforts him. While it is true that he will be cast out ("become the thirteenth") and cursed, in the end he will rule over them all and ascend to the holy race.

The text in verse 30 is difficult, for it appears that the scribe made a mistake, leaving out one or more words by accident (indicated by pointed brackets). The text that remains suggests that the disciples are going to do something to Judas (perhaps stone him? — a suggestion from Stephen Emmel in conversation), after which he will ascend to the holy race.

10–14 This long section contains Jesus's revelation to Judas about the origin and shape of the universe. This is the most prominent topic in the entire gospel — it takes up more than 40 percent of the *Gospel of Judas* and dominates Jesus's teaching throughout. From the very beginning, when the gospel says that Jesus came for the salvation of humankind, we are told that he delivers that salvation by teaching people about "the mysteries which are beyond the world and the things which will occur at the end."

Yet contemporary readers may well ask: How can such teaching help anyone? Many people I have spoken with find most of it bizarre, if not simply incomprehensible. What message of any value could it possibly contain? The alien names and aeons, the strange and complicated use of numbers, and many missing parts of the ancient manuscript — all these make it difficult, if not impossible, to grasp the underlying message. Yet understanding this material is crucial, because it contains the answers to every important question in the *Gospel of Judas:* the nature of God, what it means to be human, why people suffer and die, why Jesus was crucified, why Judas handed him over, and much more.

Moreover, this kind of thinking is not as difficult to comprehend as it may first appear. Arcane as ancient cosmology may seem to contemporary readers, we are familiar with the basic concept: What we know about the universe directly relates to what we understand about human nature. We can see this kind of thinking today, for example, in the debates over evolution and intelligent design (or creationism). Here, too, people are trying in various ways to confront some of the most central issues that people in any age must face: What is the nature of reality? How did the world and humanity come into being? What is the place of humanity in the universe? Does the universe have a moral order or is it all random? What is the truth of the Bible and revelation — or, for that matter, any religious claim?

This debate illustrates how disputes over the nature of the universe often involve basic religious and philosophic questions about how to understand human nature, how people should live, and how, if at all, they are to relate to the divine. We are not dismissive of any position in this debate — neither that of scientists who defend evolution and genetics nor that of people unwilling to give up the Bible as a moral and spiritual anchor. Yet many people still wonder what the debate is really about.

They ask why some religious people object to evolutionary theory and genetics, since intelligent design lacks the scientific evidence to challenge them. Moreover, many scientists and theologians agree that religion and science are not mutually exclusive.[14] What, then, is the problem? For many, the issue is not so much what scientists say as what their theories might imply — as Pope John Paul II put it, seeing "the cosmos as the result of an evolution of matter reducible to pure chance and necessity."[15] The Dalai Lama adds that this kind of materialist philosophy would be "an invitation to nihilism and spiritual poverty."[16]

Moreover, some Christians argue against evolution because it challenges their interpretation of the Bible and its authority. For them, the fundamental values at stake are not bound to science but to particular readings of what they regard as divinely inspired Scripture. Their position excludes anything that does not accept their reading of the *Genesis* account as the authoritative framework within which science must work. Similarly, the Church's dispute with Galileo was not about his scientific views but about what some people took to be their implications for what it means to be human and how humans relate to God. In both cases, scientific theory seemed to threaten the Christian teaching that humans have a special relationship to God. No longer at the center of the universe, people seem left either to the machinations of uncaring chance or to rigid necessity.

In the *Gospel of Judas,* Jesus teaches people about the kinship they have with God and about how to live according to the moral order of the universe established by God. People, Jesus says, have spiritual resources within them beyond what they know. He explains this message by telling Judas about the nature of the universe — that another realm exists beyond the material world, and an immortal holy race above the mortal human race. If people can understand this reality, they can fulfill their highest nature and understand how they should live now. He explains that human beings were created following the divine image of the heavenly First Man, Adamas. To honor this divine image in people, God sent divine spirits to everyone, giving people the potential to turn and worship him. By looking within themselves, people can "bring forth the perfect human" — they can discover what is divine and immortal within themselves.

But people need to understand, too, how

it is that they are ignorant of this higher realm and of their own inner spiritual nature. Jesus explains that although people are made according to the divine image and likeness, they are nonetheless created by the lower angels God put in charge of the material world — the realm of chaos and oblivion. Because these angels are themselves subject to error through their own arrogance and ignorance, they have led humanity astray by getting people to worship them. They confuse some people into thinking that human beings are righteous when they perform seemingly pious acts like sacrifice, fasting, prayer, and baptism. By performing these acts, such people become hardened in their ways and, like the twelve disciples, resist Jesus's criticism, especially since — as becomes clear throughout the gospel — following Jesus does not mean gaining power and glory in this world; it means being cursed, suffering, and dying.

This theme — that Christian discipleship means following Jesus by imitating his suffering and death — is certainly not new to the *Gospel of Judas*. Already the earliest of the New Testament gospels, the *Gospel of Mark*, sounds this theme, stressing repeatedly its message of suffering discipleship. As we have seen, too, many Christians in the second century understood the death of martyrs in this way. What, then, is different in what the *Gospel of Judas* says? The author stresses that the true God does not desire this suffering and death. Indeed, Jesus is sent to demonstrate that death is only a step into eternity. Suffering and death occur only because the world rulers and those who follow them have gone astray. Yet their allotted time will come to an end, and they will all be destroyed. Such is the justice of the true God on high. Nor will bodies of flesh be raised to eternal life; the flesh belongs to the material world that is destined to fall back into the chaos out of which it came. Only false "Gods" promise that the perishable flesh can become imperishable. That is a lie. They and all those who follow them will perish, along with the world where they now rule.

Given this situation, how can people survive? In the *Gospel of Judas,* this problem is posed as an eschatological problem; Jesus talks about life and death in terms of what will happen in the end times. At stake is not merely the personal survival of people beyond the grave but the question of whether the world has a moral order, whether justice will prevail in spite of all the violence, unjust suffering, and evil that people suffer. The author of the *Gospel of Judas* affirms — against all the seeming evidence of Jesus's death, Judas's death, and the persecution of Christians in his own day — that justice does exist, that the glorious life of the spirit will triumph over every evil.

Chapters 10–14 of the *Gospel of Judas* contain the core of Jesus's teaching. Many things Jesus has only hinted at before are presented here more systematically.[17] We can best understand the thinking underlying the *Gospel of Judas* by grasping some of the core presuppositions the author assumes. The author of the *Gospel of Judas,* like other early Christians, turned first to the biblical book of *Genesis* to answer questions about human nature, moral order, and their relationship to God. But even as people today read their sacred stories in terms of what they know about science, so too ancient Christians interpreted *Genesis* in the light of ancient philosophical and scientific thinking, especially astronomy, as well as Jewish interpretations of Scripture. Ideas from all these sources appear in the *Gospel of Judas,* as we will see. Another presupposition is that the world we live in was patterned after a higher, perfect realm of God above. These Christians read *Genesis* knowing that the account of the creation of the lower world would contain hints about that heavenly realm, since this world is patterned upon it. They therefore not only read *Genesis* to learn about the nature of this world but also sought clues in it about the nature of the transcendent realm of God above. In chapters 10–11, Jesus describes that realm to Judas.

10:1 Here we learn why knowledge of the divine realm above requires a savior who comes down from above. For Judas could never comprehend the heavenly world himself, Jesus tells him here, because it is not visible to the human eye. Jesus is talking about things beyond even the highest of the visible heavens and the stars. As we will learn later, God can be known in this world — not by examining the heavens, as most people in the ancient world believed, but by looking *within.*

10:2 The heavenly realm is beyond comprehension — even by angels. It is boundless, and hence cannot be measured or limited in any way. The reader is to imagine a higher, invisible reality.

10:3–5 In this realm exists the highest God, whom Jesus calls the "Great Invisible Spirit." This great deity is beyond all comprehension — unseen, ungraspable by even the heart, such that no name can truly express its essence. Metaphorically, this realm is like a cloud — it has substance but can't be grasped; it can be seen, but what lies in it is obscure. Yet it is also light — radiant, life-giving, illuminating. This is the true God; the "spirit of God" that "moved over the face of the waters" described in *Genesis* 1:2 is but a reflection of him.

The notion that God cannot be heard, seen, or comprehended is common in Jewish and Christian literature (compare *Isaiah* 64:4; and from the Nag Hammadi texts: *Prayer of the Apostle Paul* 1:25–29; *Gospel of Thomas* 17; *Tripartite Tractate* 54:15–19), but is especially close in context to the sentiment of Paul, who writes:

Among the mature we do speak wisdom, although it is not a wisdom of this age or of the rulers of this age, who are doomed to perish. But we speak God's wisdom, secret and hidden, which God decreed before the ages for our glory. None of the rulers of this age understood this; for if they had, they would not have crucified the Lord of glory. But, as it is written, "What no eye has seen, nor ear heard, nor the human heart conceived, what God has prepared for those who love him" (*1 Corinthians* 2:6–9).

In the *Gospel of Judas,* it is Jesus who imparts secret wisdom to Judas — wisdom hidden from the rulers of this world and unknown to humanity. This revealed knowledge is contrasted with the "polluted and perishable wisdom" claimed by those who are ruled by the lower angels of this world (*Judas* 8:7).

10:6–20 As in *Genesis,* creation begins with God's command. The first to come into being is the great angel, the divine Autogenes, whose name literally means "the self-begotten." In a number of related works found in Egypt, Autogenes is associated with Christ.[18] Here he comes forth from the cloud of light. From another cloud come four angels to attend him. These form the original pentad — the five who are the highest in the divine realm. As we will see, five others are "first over chaos" below, including the highest, Seth-Christ. Thus these five provide the model for ordering the material world below.

Next, Autogenes brings forth Adamas and appoints a luminary to rule over his realm. Immeasurable myriads are created to worship the highest, most luminous being in each realm of light. This pattern is important, for it indicates that ruling is crucial to the divine order. Each being is set in its proper place; the higher rule over the lesser, who are appointed to attend and serve them. Thus the pattern of ruling and serving is established as one that is not only good and natural but divine. The entire universe was ordered this way by God's command — both the divine realm above and the world below. Ruling and order display God's goodness.

11:1–12 Jesus returns to focus more closely upon the figure of Adamas. His elevated status is emphasized — he dwells in the first cloud, which is so transcendent that not even the angels are able to see it. Here the author comments ironically that the supposed "gods" of this world are unable to perceive the higher realms above — in this case, the luminous "cloud" of Adamas.

Adamas, who is the heavenly model for the human Adam described in *Genesis* 5:3, brings forth a child in his image and likeness, Seth, and with Seth an imperishable race comes to exist. The numbers twelve and twenty-four appear for the first time, but it is not clear exactly what they refer to, because of the missing text. Through an act of will, Adamas brought forth seventy-two luminaries. Each of those brought forth five additional luminaries, for a total of 360.

Jesus explains that the "father" — the origin and ruler — of the others is the twelve luminaries and their realms, each with six heavens, to create a total of seventy-two heavens for the same number of luminaries. These seventy-two each had five firmaments, bringing the total again to 360. All these were given authority over an innumerable army of angels, not to mention over additional virginal spirits, who were created to glorify and worship them.[19]

Why the repeated emphasis on numbers? For the *Gospel of Judas,* numbers are evidence of the Invisible Spirit's true nature. They show divine goodness by demonstrating the orderliness of creation, and in the world below they provide visible evidence of God's existence. (For more on numbers, see note to 12:5–21). All these luminaries and angels, in their mathematical order, form the shape of the immaterial, spiritual world of light above. They also provide the model for the subsequent creation of the material world below. As we will see, the stars and planets of the visible heavens come into being as a material reflection of eternity.

Properly read, then, Scripture reveals something of this divine world. The movement of the Spirit at creation, the voice of God calling the universe into existence, the heavenly luminaries — so like the sun, moon, and stars below — each ruling its own sphere, the appearance of the heavenly Adam, his son Seth (and, as we will see, Eve), along with the whole heavenly race: All these can be seen as the true models of what will come into being in the material cosmos that Jesus describes in chapter 12–13.

12:1–3 Jesus now introduces a new topic: the creation of the perishable world, the cosmos. He begins by stressing it was by the will of the Father above and his highest angels that the First Human, Adamas, accompanied by all his imperishable powers, appeared in the lower, material world. That realm contained the race of Adamas, along with the cloud of knowledge and the angel El; these appear to be references to the material world as a kind of earthly paradise that contains (the tree of) knowledge and where El walks and the race of Adam is born. We see here, then, the beginning of the account of the creation of the lower world, but with a clear emphasis on elements of its divine character. In contrast to other Christian works like *The Secret Revelation of John,* in which the creation of the world is accomplished by fallen angels acting *against* God's will, here everything is ordered according to God's will.

12:5–21 It is not clear who is speaking here and creating the lower-world angels — perhaps Autogenes. We see him now bringing forth angels to rule over "chaos and the oblivion," the formless void described in *Genesis* 1:2. We are not told where this realm came from; it is simply there, following the ancient belief that a dead, formless matter existed as a kind of dark chaos before God gave it form and life. God's goodness thus consists in setting limits on its turbulent and destructive essence, bringing some kind of light and purpose into the dark void by establishing angelic beings to rule over it.

Twelve angels come into being to rule over the chaos. The first has a face of fire — reminiscent of divine light, but this likeness is the color of blood, showing that his "light" is defiled; it consumes rather than illumines. His name, Nebro, also tells us about his character, for it is interpreted as "apostate," leading one immediately to think of fallen angels like Satan.

Next comes Saklas with six other angels to attend him — just as the divine luminaries above had angels to serve and worship them. These allotted a portion in the heavens to another twelve angels. And finally five rulers come into being over oblivion — modeled after Autogenes and his four angels, who preside over the divine realm. The first of those lowest angels has two names: Seth and Christ.

Strange as it may seem, this description conforms very closely to widespread ancient thinking about the structure of the heavens. Certain followers of Plato argued, for example, that astronomy was the one essential science for those seeking to attain true wisdom and piety.[20] Ancient astronomers envisioned a geocentric universe in which the earth appeared as a stable, unmoving sphere, around which the sun, moon, and stars revolved. Starting from this assumption, they developed sophisticated mathematical formulas to chart the movement of the celestial bodies. Like physicists and astronomers today, mathematicians in ancient times noted that they could describe the movement of the moon, stars, and planets, as well as their relationships, with numbers. Does this mean that numbers are simply an efficient language to describe the matter and energy of the universe? Or does the universe itself conform to mathematical relationships? Mathematicians from Pythagoras to Albert Einstein have speculated that numbers describe universal principles, including the shape and movement of the heavenly bodies.

Ancient scientists held that the sun is predominant, since its movement determines the cycles of night and day, as well as the seasons of the year. They recognized, too, that the earth's closest luminary, the moon, determines the pattern of the months. They gave special notice to five other stars that seemed to move irregularly, since from any fixed point of observation on Earth, Jupiter, Saturn, Mars, Mercury, and Venus (Uranus, Neptune, and the dwarf Pluto were not visible to the naked eye) looked as if they were progressing forward and then turning backward in their courses. Because of this irregularity, ancient observers often called these stars "planets," taking the term from the Greek verb *planeō* which means to "err" or "wander." By the time the *Gospel of Judas* was written, however, astronomers had realized that this term was a misnomer, since they observed that the courses of the planets were regular, although opposite to those of the stars. Ancient astronomers apportioned places to the myriad other stars, which appear to move in fixed patterns, by dividing the visible heavens into twelve parts, which we know as the zodiac. They calculated the standard year as one of 360 days, although this required occasional adjustment to account for an additional five and a quarter days every year.

In this way, philosophers and scientists conceived of numbers both as establishing principles of order and as marking intervals of time and setting boundaries in space. And while they used astronomic data for practical matters, including navigation and seasonal agricultural activities, they also regarded the harmony and stability of the heavens as proof of divine order and purpose. Ancient astronomers believed that mathematical descriptions of the universe prove that divine intelligence, not chance or necessity, pervades the universe. A work written by a later Platonist, titled the *Epinomis,* even calls numbers "the cause of all good things."[21]

The author of the *Gospel of Judas,* too, relies on numbers to demonstrate the orderliness of God's creation. He uses the numerical relationships of the heavenly world to establish the pattern for the creation of our lower cosmos with its twelve months, heavenly zodiac, and 360-day year. Judging from their descriptions and numbers, we can probably associate these beings with the sun (Nebro with his face of fire), the seven-day week (Saklas and his six attendants), the zodiac (twelve, each governing a portion of heaven), and the five planets (set over chaos). The author of the *Gospel of Judas* takes the correlation between our cosmos and these heavenly numbers to prove not only that there is a world above but that divine purpose pervades the world in which we live.

These views were also confirmed by the way the author of the *Gospel of Judas* reads the creation accounts in *Genesis.* According to *Genesis* 1:3–8, God brought forth light, separating night and day, and created the firmament of heaven to divide above and below. He brought forth the sun, moon, and stars and established them as signs for seasons, days, and years, and to rule over day and night. When he was finished, "God saw that it was good" (*Genesis* 1:14–18). In this way, the *Gospel of Judas* shows that the true God is ultimately responsible for the whole universe, both the heavens above and the world below. Our world is a continuation of God's creation of the world above.

Because of the high regard for the heavenly bodies, many people in the ancient Mediterranean world regarded the stars as living, even divine, beings — led by gods, some said, or images of gods. They offered sacrifices and devoted festivals to these astral deities, and they especially revered the sun.

Because the *Gospel of Judas* identifies the rulers of the lower world with the heavenly bodies, he is accusing Jesus's disciples of worshipping astral deities when they "sacrifice" Jesus and martyrs to Saklas. "Cease sacrificing," Jesus commands them.

This author is not alone in denouncing the science of astronomy as well as the popular reverence for stars and planets, for certain philosophers, as well as many Jews and Christians, did so as well. Plutarch, for example, said that many people dismissed astronomers because "they frittered away divinity into irrational causes, unforeseen forces, and necessary occurrences."[22] Not unlike opponents of science today, Plato had warned that natural philosophy leads to atheism, because it suggests "that the world had come into being not by mind, God, or skill, but by nature and chance."[23] Jews and Christians who relied on *Genesis,* which describes the sun, moon, planets, and stars as natural phenomena that God created, opposed the notion that the stars were living gods. Instead, many Jews insisted, the one true God had created all these heavenly bodies and appointed angels to rule over them. Christians, too, attributed everything to God's providence and free will, so that whenever celestial events appeared as signs, they indicated only what God intended them to show — that God's purpose was at work in the life of Jesus, as, for example, when it was claimed that an especially brilliant star led the Magi to Jesus's birthplace or that an eclipse of the sun occurred at the time of his death or when Christians prophesied that heavenly events would announce his return.[24] Those who believe the astrologers fail to see that God rules over these heavenly signs, the church father Origen said, so that in effect "the determinism presupposed by astrology would empty all meaning out of Christ's redemption, the efforts of the apostles, human endeavor, and prayer, and would make God unjust."[25]

The author of the *Gospel of Judas* agrees. The movement of the heavenly bodies follows God's plan — it is the stars that will bring everything to completion (*Judas* 14:2–5). Yet at the same time the stars can lead people astray. Jesus refers to Judas's star twice, in ways that seem contradictory: "Your star is leading you astray," he says, when Judas wrongly interprets his dream about the heavenly temple above (*Judas* 9:15). But later Jesus tells Judas, "The star that leads the way, that is your star" (*Judas*

15:16). Contradictory as this appears, we see at work one of the *Gospel of Judas's* main assumptions: that the heavenly bodies are set in place by God, but nonetheless they can go astray and err. Where does this notion come from?

Partly it derives from observation of the planets, who seem to "err" in their courses. But the more accurate answer with regard to the *Gospel of Judas* is that although the angels in charge of the world were created and appointed by God, they are deficient beings, because they share in the nature of the lower realm over which they rule. Unlike the angels in heaven above, these beings are mortal. They are limited in other ways as well: God set terms for their rule, and allowed them only limited understanding as well, for as we have seen, they also can err and lead people astray.

This portrait of the angelic world rulers draws much from the kind of thinking we find in Jewish apocalyptic literature, most of which was written later than the books of the Hebrew Bible but before the beginning of Christianity. For example, a book ascribed to the great prophet Enoch describes how the exact computation of the times and seasons was revealed to him by Uriel, the angel who has "the power in the heaven over both day and night so that he may cause the light to shine over the people — sun, moon, and stars, and all the principalities of the heaven which revolve in their (respective) circuits" (*1 Enoch* 82).[26] Uriel explains that God appointed angelic leaders and captains over each of the four seasons, the twelve months, and the 360 days, along with the names, orders, and the subordinates of those captains over thousands. As in the *Gospel of Judas,* these angels are imperfect; sometimes they err, and even lead humanity into error:

Many of the chiefs of the stars shall make errors in respect to the orders given to them; they shall change their courses and functions and not appear during the seasons which have been prescribed for them. All the orders of the stars shall harden (in disposition) against the sinners and the conscience of those that dwell upon the earth. They (the stars) shall err against them (the sinners); and modify all their courses. Then they (the sinners) shall err and take them (the stars) to be gods. And evil things shall be multiplied upon them; and plagues shall come upon them, so as to destroy all (*1 Enoch* 80:6–8).

1 Enoch teaches here that errant angels can cause violence and false worship among human beings. Such is also the nature of the angels God appoints to rule the world in the *Gospel of Judas*. Jesus tells Judas how God brought order to the lower, material world by placing it under the rule of these lower angels for a limited time.

13:1–7 Here we learn that it was Saklas and his angels who created humanity. They formed Adam and Eve according to the image and likeness of the divine world above. But because these erring angels are the "Gods" who formed Adam and Eve, humanity lives under their rule and shares their character flaws and their mortal nature. Not only are people capable of unrighteousness and error; their lifespans are also limited, as Saklas told them: "Your life and that of your children will last (only) for a season." It is likely that the missing portion of the text at 13:6 contained Saklas's command not to eat of the tree of paradise, following the story in *Genesis* 2:15–17 and 3:1–24. There, God commands Adam not to eat of the tree of the knowledge of good and evil, but when Eve and Adam do eat of it, God casts them out of paradise lest they should eat of the tree of life and live forever. The consequence in both *Genesis* and the

Gospel of Judas is the same: All human beings now have limited lifespans.

This reading of *Genesis* may seem to conflict with the literal meaning of the text, but it does solve several problems that ancient readers had, and it conforms to the highest philosophical standards of its time. Jews and Christians in this period were all struggling with certain problems in *Genesis,* notably the portrait of God as a limited being who "walks in the garden in the cool of the day" and has to ask Adam and Eve where they were — as though he didn't know. They also had to account for the plural in *Genesis* 1:26, where God says, "let *us* make humankind in *our* image." Who is this "we" if there is only one true God? Portraying the creator as Saklas and his angelic friends solved the problems for the author of the *Gospel of Judas.*

Moreover, the *Gospel of Judas* draws on the thinking of Plato and his followers. Offering his own version of the story of creation, Plato suggested that the transcendent God delegated the task of forming the material world to a lower creator, called the Demiurge, and to "the younger gods" who were with him. In creating this world, they looked to the eternal, spiritual realm above and stamped its form upon the chaotic matter with which they had to work, giving order and beauty to all that they made. The immortal souls of humans originally resided in the stars, a vantage point from which they could comprehend the whole cosmos. But when the lower gods placed them into human bodies, they forgot everything they had known before. Plato tells this story to teach his students what he sees as the goal of human life: to remember the truth about ourselves and our origin, so that when death releases the righteous soul from the prison of the body, it can return to the immortal stars and regain the knowledge of the universe that it originally had — the memory that we lost to oblivion when we were born into this world.[27]

The *Gospel of Judas* — and indeed most Christian views of the universe — drew heavily upon the philosophy of Plato and his followers. Many Christians accepted the dualistic view that human beings are souls residing in physical bodies. Like Plato, they understood God as a transcendent Being far beyond the material world of chaos and death, a Being who relegated contact with the material world to lower angels.

13:8–10 As soon as Jesus reveals that Saklas has limited the human lifespan, Judas immediately wants to know how long people can live. But again Jesus rebukes him: "Why are you surprised that the lifespan of Adam and his race is numbered in this place? It is in this place that he received his kingdom, with its ruler, for a (limited) number." Again, Judas does not yet grasp that anything that lives in the world below is destined to perish at the end of time. The lifespans of Adam and his race are limited on earth. God appointed Adam (and his children) to rule here (i.e., "he received his kingdom, in this place"), following *Genesis* 1:28, in which God gives Adam dominion over the earth and every living thing in it. But Jesus points out to Judas that this place also has its ruler — Saklas, for according to *Genesis* 1:16–18, God gave the rule of the heavens over to the heavenly luminaries. So both the lifespan of human beings and their dominion on earth is *numbered* (given a fixed measure). By referring twice to Adam's life and rule being literally "in a number," the author stresses again that everything that happens follows a mathematical reckoning set by the true God above, even in the world of chaos and oblivion, since all number and orderliness ultimately comes from the true God. In this case, the numbers set limits both upon human lifespan and upon dominion over the earth. Jesus now has to make it clear to Judas that this dominion was not meant to be permanent. It is only temporary — and that should come as no surprise to Judas given what Jesus has just revealed to him about the origin of the world.

13:11–17 Judas's next question, "Does the human spirit die?," shows that he is beginning to understand. The body will die and the world will perish, but the spirit does not belong to this perishable realm but to the world above. What will happen to it at the end of time? The divine spirit cannot perish, but the *Gospel of Judas* assumes the death of the physical body and its finality. Moreover, it teaches that even souls are mortal unless they are joined with immortal spirits. Jesus has already told Judas that the souls of everyone who belongs solely to the human race will die (8:2). But here Judas asks about the spirit, not the body or the soul. Jesus's answer to his question is complex. He says that God commanded the angel Michael only to loan spirits to human beings, so that they might worship God for the time allotted to their kingdom (with its ruler). But when that time is over, their worship comes to an end and they die (body and soul). But, Jesus says, others receive a spirit from another angel, Gabriel, so that when their bodies die, their souls remain alive and are lifted up to the heavenly realm. These received the spirits of the great undominated race: that is to say, spirits from the kingdom above, where the rulers of chaos cannot lord over them. Those with immortal spirits will dwell above forever in the holy place reserved for them (8:3–4; 13:12–13). Thus, in the end, the souls of those who worship the angelic rulers of the lower world perish along with them, while the souls of those who turn toward the world above remain united with the spirit and are lifted up to join the holy race on high.

Although throughout the gospel Jesus speaks about *two* races — the mortal and immortal — making it sound like people are predestined for either death or eternal life, that is not an accurate reading of the *Gospel of Judas.* Rather, what we see are two perspectives intertwined. From the viewpoint of the final judgment at the end of time, people can be divided into these two groups. As Jesus explains it, all people have received spirits from God, but some people only have them on "loan," while others possess spirits of the "great undominated race." Although this sounds deterministic, he goes on to call upon souls to seek the spirit within. People, Jesus teaches, are the ones who cause the spirit to dwell in the flesh, for God gave humanity (Adam and those with him) the knowledge they need to escape the domination of the world rulers. Thus Jesus makes it clear that everyone is created in the image of the divine Adamas, and everyone has a spirit from God. Whether they lose their divine spirits when they die or whether they ascend to the eternal realm above depends on what they do in this life. If people turn inward and come to know their inner spirit, they surpass the rule of the lower angels, and when their bodies perish, their souls live on with the immortal spirit given by God. If, however, they refuse to follow Jesus's teaching and persist in their false piety, following the violent path of the world rulers, at death they perish entirely, bodies and souls, for their spirits leave them as they ascend back to God. So from the perspective of the present time, salvation is a possibility for everyone. The true nature of individuals — whether they belong to the mortal human race or the great undominated race — will only become clear at the end.

14:1–18 When the appointed time comes, Jesus tells him, the erring stars and planetary rulers will be destroyed, along with everything they have created, as has been prophesied. All the people who follow them will collapse into moral chaos, killing their own children and engaging in violence and sexual transgression (*Judas* 14:2–7, 14–16). These are the signs of the end (cf. also *Judas* 5:8–16).

Many other Christians then as now shared the conviction that the end time would be an era of violent destruction. According to the *Gospel of Mark,* the signs of the end appear when people see the order of creation reversed: "The sun will be darkened, and the moon will not give its light, and the stars will be falling from heaven, and the powers in the heavens will be shaken" (*Mark* 13:24–25). *1 John* claims that "the whole world lies under the power of the evil one" (5:19), and the longest apocalyptic prophecy in the New Testament, in the *Book of Revelation,* predicts a great war in heaven before the final destruction of the world. Satan and his angels temporarily rule over the world, and it is they who inspire rulers to kill Jesus and to make war upon his followers. John, the prophet of *Revelation,* also takes astrological signs as omens of God's divine plan.[28] The *Book of Revelation,* like the *Gospel of Judas,* depicts Jesus teaching that the present world is about to be destroyed, along with all who worship the demonic powers that now hold power. All of these "books of revelation" claim that in the end, only believers will be saved. The *Gospel of Mark* writes that the Son of Man will "send out the angels, and gather his elect from the four winds, from the ends of the earth to the ends of heaven" (*Mark* 13:27). *1 John* insists that "the Son of God has come and has given us understanding so that we may know him who is true," leading believers from idolatry to eternal life (*1 John* 5:20–21). In *Revelation,* only believers gain eternal life in the new creation, a heavenly Jerusalem descended from heaven (*Revelation* 21), while unbelievers are condemned to eternal punishment in the lake of fire (*Revelation* 20:15).

The *Gospel of Judas* expresses the same conviction, teaching that this world will not long endure and that all those on earth who ignore Jesus's teaching will die. When Jesus laughs again, we learn that the stars and planets that rule the heavens and the lower realm of chaos will all be destroyed, along with everything they have created (*Judas* 14:16).

Judas asks about those who are baptized in his name, but unfortunately Jesus's answer is lost in a hole in the text. We can speculate, however, that his answer might have resembled what we hear in the *Testimony of Truth:* "There are some, who upon entering the faith, receive a baptism on the ground that they have [it] as a hope of salvation . . . (but) the Son of Man did not baptize any of his disciples. For [. . . if those who] are baptized were headed for life, the world would become empty. . . . But the baptism of truth is something else; it is by renunciation of the world that it is found. [But those who] say [only] with the tongue [that they] are renouncing it [are lying], and they are coming to [the place] of fear" (*Testimony of Truth* 69:7–29). No pious act brings salvation; only turning away from "the world" and its rulers to God above.

Jesus explains to Judas, "Your star will rule over the thirteenth realm" (*Judas* 14:11). Some scholars have taken this to mean that Judas will surpass the lower twelve rulers of the world, and come to dwell in a realm above them, but still be outside the realm of the heavenly temple above. Clearly, the number thirteen signals Judas and those who follow his star will ascend above the domination of the world's rulers and escape destruction. It does not seem, however, that this thirteenth realm is the final resting place for Judas, since Jesus clearly teaches that those who are of the immortal holy race will dwell in the divine realms above. The key passage is above in *Judas* 15:12–13.

15:1–4 This passage prophesies the destruction of all those who sacrifice to Saklas. Judas will surpass them all when he "sacrifice(s) the human who bears (Jesus)." As we discussed above, this sacrifice is meant as a demonstration that the true spiritual nature of humanity is not flesh, nor can it be constrained by death. Thus, while "the human" who bears Jesus is mortal flesh and truly suffered and died, this mortal human was never the final reality about Jesus, who is in essence a divine spiritual being — like all other people who possess the immortal spirit. Although it is a bit speculative, to us the point in the *Gospel of Judas* seems to be that Jesus represents the true nature of all human beings who worship the true God. Their fleshly bodies are real; they suffer and die; but at the same time, their true nature is the spirit-filled soul, which will live forever with God above. We might call this a kind of "docetism" (that is, from the Greek verb *dokeo*, "to seem," the view that Jesus only *seemed* to have a real body of flesh and blood that in fact was just an appearance) but with the very strong caveat that the human body is real — really suffers and dies. It is no apparition but merely mortal.

15:5–13 Here we see images of Judas as the prophet of the end time. Images of a horn raised up and ready to be sounded, of anger, sidereal omens, and the victory of the heart — all these are common signs of the end times. Judas's act in handing Jesus over is the beginning of the end, of the lapse of humankind into moral chaos. Perhaps the author of *Judas* thought that he was living in the last days, seeing the signs of the end in the death of Christians at the hands of the Romans and in the condemnation of all those like him by fellow Christians who were offering sacrifice to Saklas (through the deaths of martyrs) as we have seen.

But here, too, Jesus teaches Judas that after the final destruction is complete, the place where the great race of Adam dwells — perhaps the realm of the thirteenth — will be exalted. Because that race existed before the lower angels came into being and before the lower heaven and earth were created, members of Adam's race will escape destruction and be elevated to the realm above.

15:14–20 Finally, Judas comprehends the full meaning of Jesus's teaching. "Everything has been told to you," Jesus tells him. He instructs Judas to lift up his eyes — no longer does he need to avert them as he did at the beginning of the gospel. Now Judas is able to perceive the divine realm above. He sees the stars there — these "stars" are perhaps the luminous spirits given to every human being at birth — now residing above in the luminous cloud. How is it that Judas's star leads the way? It is because he is now able to enter into the luminous cloud. This scene shows that even while people live in the body, it is possible to know God.

16:1–9 The final scene of the *Gospel of Judas* appears to stage the moment in the story, like that in the *Gospel of John,* when Jesus has told Judas to go and do what he has to, as Stephen Emmel has pointed out.[29] Jesus (with his disciples?) has entered the "guest room" of the Temple, like the guest room of the house where Jesus prepares for Passover with his disciples in other gospels (the same term, *kataluma,* is used in *Mark* 14:14 and *Luke* 22:11). Some scribes are waiting outside, hoping to catch him away from the crowds that follow him (as Judas does, according to *Luke* 22:6), because those crowds consider him to be a holy prophet. Judas, too, is standing outside and the scribes approach him, recognizing that he is one of Jesus's intimate followers. Judas then takes the money and hands Jesus over. The gospel comes to an end.

Christian readers of the second century surely knew how the story continued: that Jesus was arrested, tried, and put to death but rose from the dead and ascended into heaven. For the *Gospel of Judas,* however, everything necessary has already been said, for it is Jesus's teaching that brings eternal life, not his death or even his resurrection. They merely demonstrate the truth of what he has told Judas: that while the body perishes, the spirit is alive in God.

When the *Gospel of Judas* was first published, newspapers and other media announced that it would undermine Christian anti-Judaism by rehabilitating Judas (whose name is related to the word *Jew*). No longer the betrayers of Christ, Jews would be free from that slander at last. But while the *Gospel of Judas* does give a positive face to Judas's act of handing Jesus over, it also portrays the Jewish chief priests and scribes as the ones who are waiting to catch Jesus. No hint appears that the Romans — who actually put Jesus to death — played any role at all. All blame is placed squarely on the Jews — those scribes who pay Judas to hand Jesus over and even Jesus's own disciples, who are portrayed as killers and sinners standing at the altar of the Jerusalem Temple. This ending offers no redemption for Jewish-Christian relations, but it does call us to reconsider how the (largely unhistorical) portrait of Judas in the gospels and many other unhistorical features of the gospel story need to be corrected.[30] Whether people accept or reject what the *Gospel of Judas* says, it should be approached in terms of what we can learn about the historical situation of the Christians who wrote and read it: their anger, their prejudices, their fears — and their hopes.

INDEX OF
CROSS-REFERENCES

When the *Gospel of Judas* was first studied, scholars numbered it according to the page and line numbers of the manuscript (the Tchacos Codex). Since the *Gospel of Judas* starts on page 33 and ends on page 58, the first number was 33. While these numbers are helpful for scholars reading the actual Coptic manuscript, they are confusing to the general reader, since the numbering doesn't follow the literary shape of the gospel; indeed, pages can end and begin even in the middle of sentences. I have therefore made a new numbering system in chapter and verse numbers that follows the literary structure of the work. This is complicated, however, in cases where whole passages are missing; in these cases I have simply added a chapter or verse number to mark the loss of several lines. For those who wish to cross reference the Coptic manuscript with the translation given here, the following index can be used as a guide.

Tchacos Codex Manuscript page number	English Translation
33	1:1–2:2a
34	2:2b–15a
35	2:15b–28
36	2:29–3:7
37	3:8–4:4
38	4:5–15
39	4:16–5:4
40	5:4–16
41	5:17–6:??
42	6:??–7:??
43	7:??–8:6
44	8:6–9:8
45	9:8–20
46	9:21–30
47	9:30–10:10
48	10:10–23
49	10:23–11:10
50	11:10–12:3
51	12:3–14
52	12:14–13:6
53	13:6–14
54	13:14–14:7
55	14:8–18
56	14:18–15:8
57	15:9–20
58	15:20–16:10

NOTES

ON READING JUDAS

Introduction

1. For more on the discovery and restoration of the Tchacos Codex, see *The Gospel of Judas,* by Rodolphe Kasser, Marvin Meyer, and Gregor Wurst, editors (Washington, DC: National Geographic, 2006), esp. pp. 11–16, 47–76; Herbert Krosney, *The Lost Gospel: The Quest for the Gospel of Judas Iscariot* (Washington, DC: National Geographic, 2006).

2. Irenaeus, *Against Heresies* 1.31.1. All references to *Against Heresies* are from the critical edition of Adelin Rousseau and Louis Doutreleau, *Irénée de Lyon, Contre les heresies,* 5 vols. (Paris: Les Éditions de Cerf, 1979); English translation (sometimes modified) from A. Cleveland Coxe, *The Apostolic Fathers with Justin Martyr and Irenaeus, vol. 1* of *The Ante-Nicene Fathers*

(Grand Rapids, MI: Eerdmans, 1885 [reprint 1979]). Available online at www.early christianwritings.com.

The *Gospel of Judas* is also mentioned by Epiphanius in his *Panarion* 38.1.5, but his report is probably based upon Irenaeus. See the discussion of the *Gospel of Judas* in Wilhelm Schneemelcher, editor, *New Testament Apocrypha. Vol. 1: Gospels and Related Writings,* Louisville, KY: Westminster/John Knox Press, 1991, pp. 386–387. Gregor Wurst makes the convincing argument that the newly discovered *Gospel of Judas* is a Coptic translation of the Greek original mentioned by Irenaeus (see "Irenaeus of Lyon and the Gospel of Judas" in *The Gospel of Judas,* Rodolphe Kasser, Marvin Meyer, and Gregor Wurst, editors, Washington, DC: National Geographic, 2006, pp. 121–135).

3. For the story of this find and a collection of these works in English translation, see *The Nag Hammadi Library in English,* James M. Robinson and Richard Smith, editors. Third edition (San Francisco: Harper and Row, 1988).

4. Let me give just one example. One scholar writes that "Judas was the only one who could do what Jesus needed: Turn him over to the authorities that he might be killed and escape his temporary entrapment

in a mortal body" (Bart Ehrman, *The Lost Gospel of Judas Iscariot: A New Look at Betrayer and Betrayed,* New York: Oxford University Press, 2006, p. 172). This statement presupposes that Gnostics hated the body and the world and considered them to be evil; the Savior thus supposedly came to free people from the prison of the body but became trapped himself and needed someone to save him (a view often referred to as the "saved Savior"). In this case, supposedly it was Judas who saved the entrapped Jesus. But according to the *Gospel of Judas,* Jesus was never trapped in the mortal body. The author tells us that at least once during his ministry he left the disciples and went up to visit the heavenly world (*Judas* 3:4) — and indeed, not only Jesus, but Judas too is able to gaze upon that heavenly world and enter it, before either of them is killed. What, then, is the point of the betrayal if it is not so-called Gnostic redemption from the body? For the *Gospel of Judas,* the point is that the glorious life of the spirit transcends the suffering and violence of this troubled world, and that it is possible to live that life here and now. What we learn from the *Gospel of Judas* is the true nature of God and the world, what it means to be fully human, fully divine. Imposing the

Gnostic redeemer myth onto the *Gospel of Judas* distorts the text and complicates attempts to understand what is at stake in how it presents Jesus and Judas.

Multiple examples of this kind of distortion could be given (e.g., in claiming that the Savior comes to save "the divine spark" that belongs by nature to a select group of people irrespective of their moral lives; or that salvation comes through *gnosis;* etc.) based in part on the author's method. He argues that it is appropriate to read *into* the text views that are not there, under the supposition that these ideas would have been presupposed by the author and his readers (see pp. 101–102). For a fuller history of the invention of Gnosticism, see Karen L. King, *What Is Gnosticism?* (Cambridge, MA: Belknap Press, 2003).

5. See the excellent discussion of the *Gospel of Judas* by Eduard Iricinschi, Lance Jenott, Philippa Townsend, "The Betrayer's Gospel," in *The New York Review of Books,* vol. 53, number 10, June 8, 2006. The authors proposed that the portrait of the disciples here "is a criticism of the bishops' endorsement of martyrdom, and the consequent acceptance by early Christians of execution by the Roman authorities. The author of the *Gospel of Judas* apparently

views martyrdom as a vain sacrifice, and blames the church leaders for leading their congregations like sheep to the slaughter."

6. Our sincere thanks to Chris Wilbur for this insight (forum at Church of Our Savior, Arlington, MA, June 11, 2006).

7. See Tertullian, *On Fleeing Persecution 3.6,* English translation available at www.earlychristianwritings.com/Tertullian/html.

8. These new works include not only the *Gospel of Judas* and another new work, called *The Stranger (Allogenes),* from the Tchacos Codex, but also works from the Nag Hammadi Codices, the Berlin Codex, the *Gospel of the Saviour,* and others. For English translations of many of these works, see *The Nag Hammadi Library in English,* James M. Robinson and Richard Smith, editors. (San Francisco: Harper and Row, 1988); Robert J. Miller, ed., *The Complete Gospels.* (Santa Rosa, CA: Polebridge Press, 1992); Bentley Layton, *The Gnostic Scriptures* (Garden City, NY: Doubleday, 1987). Charles W. Hedrick and Paul A. Mirecki, *Gospel of the Savior* (Santa Rosa, CA: Polebridge Press, 1999).

9. The portrait here relies upon the excellent recent discussion of Christianity in Rome by Peter Lampe, *From Paul to Valenti-*

nus: Christians at Rome in the First Two Centuries (Minneapolis, MN: Fortress Press, 2003).

Chapter One: Judas: Betrayer or Favored Disciple?

1. All quotations from the Bible are cited from the *New Revised Standard Version.*

2. *Against Heresies* 3.11.9.

3. *Against Heresies* 3.11.8.

4. "Other sides," for there were not only two sides in the debate, but multiple points of view. Irenaeus works hard to make it sound as though there were — the right one against all the wrong ones. But historians now can see that those views that came to constitute "orthodoxy" also contain many perspectives and differences of opinions. But they are differences that in some sense didn't make a difference — either theologians were able to reconcile different views by various means or else the differences were not perceived as significant.

5. For further discussion of such views of Christian polemicists, see Karen L. King, *What is Gnosticism?* (Cambridge, MA: Belknap Press, 2003), pp. 22–38.

6. *Against Heresies* 1.10.

7. *Against Heresies* 4.26.2–5. For discussion, see Elaine Pagels, *The Gnostic Gospels*

(New York: Random House, 1979), pp. 103–151. For a more recent discussion of Irenaeus's view of "canon of truth" and baptism, see Elaine Pagels, "Irenaeus, the 'Canon of Truth,' and the Gospel of John: 'Making a Difference' through Hermeneutics and Ritual," in *Vigiliae Christianae* Vol. 56, Number 4, 2002, pp. 339–371.

8. *Against Heresies* 1.20.1; praef.1–3.

9. *Apocalypse of Peter* 79.22–31.

10. Josephus, *Antiquities of the Jews, Books 18–19,* translated by L. H. Feldman, Loeb Classical Library edition, vol. 9 (Cambridge, MA: Harvard University Press, 1965), sect. 18.63.

11. Tacitus, *Annals,* translated by J. Jackson, Loeb Classical Library edition (Cambridge, MA: Harvard Unviersity Press, 1931).

12. Origen, *Against Celsus* 5.62.

13. Textual scholars argue that the *Gospel of Mark* ended at 16:8 when the women flee the tomb and say nothing, because some of the most ancient texts end there, while others add endings that differ from each other.

14. The author of the *Gospel of Luke,* who also wrote the *Acts of the Apostles,* includes a different story of Judas's unfortunate death too; See *Acts* 1:18.

15. *Acts* 1:19 also talks about the "Field

of Blood," but says that it was the field Judas bought with the money he gained betraying Jesus. According to *Acts,* it was called a "field of blood," not because it was bought with blood money but because when Judas died "he burst open in the middle and all his bowels gushed out" (*Acts* 1:18).

16. For discussion and references, see Raymond E. Brown, *The Birth of the Messiah* (New York: Doubleday, 1993). See also the work of Jane Schaberg, *The Illegitimacy of Jesus: A Feminist Theological Interpretation of the Infancy Narratives* (Sheffield, England: Sheffield Phoenix Press, 1995).

17. The Greek omits "bread"; see *Matthew* 26:23.

18. See John Dominic Crossan's discussion in *Who Killed Jesus? Exposing the Roots of Anti-Semitism in the Gospel Story of the Death of Jesus* (San Francisco, CA: HarperSanFrancisco, 1996), pp. 1–38.

19. See *Isaiah* 53:6, in the Greek translation known as the Septuagint (LXX). Thanks to Helmut Koester for this reference, from a private letter dated June 2006. Scholars hold that the New Testament authors knew the Old Testament scriptures only in Greek translation.

20. See, for example, Burton Mack's discussion in *A Myth of Innocence: Mark and*

Christian Origins (Philadelphia, PA: Fortress Press, 1988), esp. pp. 271, 292–293, 325–331. He argues that the Judas story belongs to Christian hostility toward Judaism.

21. This is the position in Crossan, *Who Killed Jesus?* pp. 69–75. He argues that Judas was a historical follower of Jesus who betrayed him but was not one of "the twelve," a designation that developed later. So, too, the increasingly negative portrait of Judas is created by Christian authors, and adds to the anti-Jewish tone and polemics of the passion narrative.

22. For discussion of the way each of the New Testament gospel writers tells the passion narrative in relation to the Jewish community of his time, see Elaine Pagels, *The Origin of Satan* (New York: Random House, New York, 1995).

Chapter Two: Judas and the Twelve

1. The source of this late tradition is the fourth-century church historian Eusebius (see *Church History* 2:1). The status of James and the Jerusalem church is now being hotly questioned. See esp. Merrill P. Miller, " 'Beginning from Jerusalem . . .': Re-examining Canon and Consensus." *Journal of Higher Criticism* 2.1 (Spring 1995), 3–30; and *Redescribing Christian Origins,* Ron

Cameron and Merrill P. Miller, editors (Atlanta: Society of Biblical Literature, 2004), pp. 141–282.

2. *Gospel of Thomas,* 114, in Elaine Pagels, *Beyond Belief* (New York: Random House, New York, 2003). All citations of the English translation of the *Gospel of Thomas* are from the appendix of *Beyond Belief.*

3. For further discussion of Mary of Magdala in these sources, including the controversies between Peter and Mary, see Karen L. King, *The Gospel of Mary of Magdala: Jesus and the First Woman Apostle* (Santa Rosa, CA: Polebridge Press, 2003), esp. pp. 83–90, 141–154. For an outstanding discussion of the historical Mary of Magdala and her portrayal in the New Testament, see Jane Schaberg with Melanie Johnson DeBanfre, *Mary Magdalene Understood* (New York: Continuum, 2006).

4. All citations of the English translation of the *Gospel of Mary* are from King, op. cit., *The Gospel of Mary of Magdala.*

5. For further discussion of traditions about Peter and Mary in conflict, see Ann Graham Brock, *Mary Magdalene, the First Apostle: The Struggle for Authority* (Cambridge, MA: Harvard University Press, 2003), esp. pp. 19–71. For an excellent examination of the ambivalent attitude

toward women in the *Gospel of Luke,* see Turid Karisen Seim, *The Double Message: Patterns of Gender in Luke-Acts* (Edinburgh: T. & T. Clark, 1994).

6. See here the discussion of Dorothy A. Lee-Pollard, "Powerlessness as Power," *The Scottish Journal of Theology,* Vol. 40, 1987, 173–88.

7. Note that Paul himself, in his letters, refers only briefly to disputes and other apostles, as in *Galatians* 1:15 and 12:2–4; the author of *Acts* gives two different — and much amplified — stories in *Acts* 9:1–23; 22:3–21.

8. Irenaeus, *Against Heresies* 1.pref; 3.12.12

9. For more on the history of Christian persecution, see W. H. C. Frend, *Martyrdom and Persecution in the Early Church: A Study of a Conflict from the Maccabees to Donatus* (Grand Rapids, MI: Baker Book House, 1965).

10. See Tertullian's vivid account of the effect of persecution, in *Scorpiace* 1.

11. Tertullian, *Apology* 7.3–4; *Ad Nationes* 7.

12. Tertullian, *Scorpiace* 1.

13. For discussion, see Elaine Pagels, "Gnostic Views of Christ's Suffering: Christian Responses to Persecution?" in Yale

Conference on Gnosticism, Vol. 1, Bentley Layton, editor, or, for a less technical discussion, see the version published in Elaine Pagels, *The Gnostic Gospels* (New York: Random House, 1979), pp. 70–101.

14. For examples of this kind, see Tertullian, *On Fleeing Martyrdom* and Ignatius, *Letter to the Romans,* where it seems that Ignatius fears the Romans may try to ransom him, for he wrote asking them not to help him: "I am voluntarily dying for God — that is, if you do not interfere. I plead with you, do not do me an unseasonable kindness" (*Ignatius Romans* 4:1; Richardson, 104). Or again: "I am going through the pangs of being born. Sympathize with me, my brothers! Do not stand in the way of my coming to life — do not wish death on me. Do not give back to the world one who wants to be God's; do not trick him with material things. Let me get into the clear light and manhood will be mine. Let me imitate the passion of my God. If anyone has Him in him, let him appreciate what I am longing for, and sympathize with me, realizing what I am going through" *(Ignatius Romans* 6:1–7:3; Richardson, *Early Christian Fathers* [New York, Collier, 1970], pp. 104–105).

15. See "The Martyrdom of Polycarp," in Musurillo, *The Acts of Christian Martyrs,* 3.

16. See "The Letter of the Churches of Lyons and Vienne," in Herbert Anthony Musurillo, *The Acts of the Christian Martyrs* (Oxford, Oxford University Press, 1972), pp. 62–85.

17. Martyrdom of Polycarp, pp. 2–21; for discussion of dating, see introduction, p. xiii.

18. *Against Heresies* 3.18.5.

19. It is impossible to cover the wide range of meanings Christians have ascribed to Jesus over the centuries — and indeed continue to do. The point here is simply to make it clear that not all Christians agreed on one meaning for Jesus's death, even in the New Testament period; atonement theology (that "Jesus died for our sins") is only one view, and one which itself has received a wide diversity of interpretations. Some introductory treatments include Jaroslav Pelikan, *Jesus Thorugh the Centuries: His Place in History and Culture* (New Haven: Yale University Press, 1999).

20. Historians agree that the Romans were the executioners, although the Jewish leadership in Jerusalem may have cooperated to some extent. The gospel writers, however, were eager to shift blame from the Romans to the Jews, both because the Jews were a less dangerous target and because of grow-

ing tensions. How much of the passion narrative is historically accurate is otherwise much disputed; see the controversy between Raymond E. Brown, *The Death of the Messiah: From Gethsemane to the Grave: A Commentary on the Passion Narratives in the Four Gospels* (New York: Doubleday, 1994) and John Dominic Crossan, *Who Killed Jesus?*

21. When Tertullian discusses those who refuse to glorify martyrdom, at any rate, these are the questions he says they raise; see *Scorpiace* 4–8.

22. For further discussion of Roman religion, see Mary Beard, John North and Simon Price, *Religions of Rome, Volume 1: A History* (Cambridge: Cambridge University Press, 1998), esp. Vol. 1, pp. 36–37 on sacrifice: "Animal sacrifice was the central ritual of many religious occasions; we know enough about it from both literary and archaeological evidence to understand its main stages. In structure, though not in detail, the ritual was closely related to the Greek ritual of sacrifice. The victim was tested and checked to make sure it was suitable; precise rules controlled the choice of sex, age, colour and type of victim, in relation to the deity and the occasion. After a procession to the altar and preparatory rites, a prayer was said in which the divine recipi-

ent was named; then the victim was made 'sacred' by the placing of wine and meal on its head and it was at this moment (so it was believed) that the signs (if any) appeared in the entrails that would imply the gods' rejection of the offering. The victim had to be killed by a single blow; its *exta* (entrails) were examined by the *haruspices* [priests whose area of expertise was the interpretation of prodigies]; assuming that they were acceptable, the animal was then butchered, cooked and eventually eaten by the worshippers."

23. Compare also *Romans* 5:18–21, which doesn't explicitly mention sacrifice.

24. Although later tradition repeats this claim, we do not have early evidence to verify it historically.

25. "The Acts of Justin and Companions," in Musurillo, *Martyr Acts,* pp. 42–61

26. "The Letter of the Churches of Lyons and Vienne," in Musurillo, *Martyr Acts,* p. 81.

27. *Apology* 50.

28. For Irenaeus's indictment of those he accuses of avoiding martyrdom, see *Against Heresies* 3.18.5; for Tertullian, see *Scorpiace* 1.

29. Irenaeus, *Against Heresies,* 1, preface.

Chapter Three: Sacrifice and the Life of the Spirit

1. During the second century, "fathers of the church" show that Christians disagreed about what the eucharist meant. Bishop Ignatius, for example, declared that those he calls heretics "do not confess that the eucharist is the flesh of our savior, Jesus Christ" (*Smyrneans* 7:1); Ignatius himself insists that the cup of wine offers union with Christ's blood, and the bread with his flesh (*Philippians* 4:1); thus it becomes the "medicine of immortality, the antidote so that we should not die, but live forever" (*Ephestans* 20:2). Ignatius connects this view of the eucharist, then, with bodily resurrection and, for that matter, with bishops whose participation alone can ensure proper worship (*Smyrneans* 7–8). The author of the *Gospel of Philip* speaks as a Christian who takes the eucharistic elements symbolically ("His flesh is the *logos,* and his blood the holy spirit"), and sees the resurrection as a spiritual process, not a physical one (*Philip.* 57:3–9). Irenaeus, writing toward the end of the second century, also derides "heretics" who celebrate the eucharist, and yet do not believe in bodily resurrection, for which Irenaeus regards it as the appropriate preparatory nourishment (see *Against Her-*

esies 4.17.5–18.5: "Just as the bread, which is produced from the earth, when it receives God's invocation is no longer common bread, but the eucharist . . . so also our bodies, when they receive the eucharist, are no longer corruptible, having the hope of the resurrection to eternity."

2. See Tertullian's discussion in *Scorpiace,* where he enumerates questions like these as examples of "heretical poison" spread by dissidents who question whether God desires — or commands — martyrdom.

3. The history of this position, generally known as "the doctrine of atonement," is notoriously varied, having been interpreted and reinterpreted from the early church into the twenty-first century. Christians have thought about Jesus's death as a ransom to liberate human sinners from bondage to sin and the devil (Gregory of Nyssa and Augustine); they have talked about the way human sin offends God's honor, so Christ paid off the infinite debt owed to God with his perfect obedience unto death (Anselm); they have said that Christ's atonement is sufficient for the sins of the whole world (Aquinas), or that Christ's life and death are meant as an inspiring exemplar of love and obedience to God, intended to move people to repent of their sins and reform

their lives (Abelard); and so on. Here we try to focus on the kind of views present in the first and second centuries that the author of the *Gospel of Judas* seems to take aim against. It should be noted, too, that theologians working on the articulation of atonement theory often address exactly such concerns: How should we think about God in light of Jesus's death? For further discussion, see Paul S. Fiddes, *Past Event and Present Salvation: The Christian Idea of Atonement* (Louisville, KY: Westminster/ John Knox Press, 1989).

4. This was a common charge by Christians and Jews (see the discussion in R.P.C. Hanson, "The Christian Attitude to Pagan Religions up to the Time of Constantine the Great" *Aufsteig und Niedergang der römischen Welt,* Wolfgang Haase, editor. II. Principat 23/2 (Berlin: Walter de Gruyter, 1980), pp. 910–973, esp. pp. 925–927.

5. *Deuteronomy* 32:17.

6. For example, Paul's denunciations we saw above closely resemble those of the Jewish author of the *Wisdom of Solomon,* who charges that devotion to false gods has corrupted pagans: ". . . living in great strife . . . whether they kill children in their initiations, or celebrate secret mysteries, or hold frenzied revels with strange customs . . .

they either treacherously kill one another, or grieve one another by adultery, and all is a raging riot of blood and murder . . . and debauchery. For the worship of idols . . . is the beginning and cause and end of every evil" (*Wisdom* 14:22–27).

7. See also *Matthew* 9:13; 12:7.

8. See the discussion of Harold W. Attridge, "The Philosophical Critique of Religion Under the Early Empire" in *Aufsteig und Niedergang der römischen Welt,* Wolfgang Haas, editor. II. Principat. 16.1 (Berlin: Walter de Gruyter, 1978), pp. 45–78); R. P. C. Hanson, op. cit., esp. pp. 910–918.

9. The social critic and satirist Lucian describes what would have been a common scene of sacrifice in any city in the Roman empire: "Although . . . no one is to be allowed within the holy-water who has not clean hands, the priest himself stands there all bloody just like the Cyclops of old, cutting up the victim, removing the entrails, plucking out the heart, pouring the blood about the altar, and doing everything possible in the way of piety. To crown it all, he lights a fire and puts upon it the goat, skin and all and sheep, wool and all; and the smoke, divine and holy, mounts upward and gradually dissipates into Heaven itself" (*On*

Sacrifices 13, translated from A. M. Harmon, *Lucian,* Loeb Classical Library edition, Vol. III. [Cambridge, MA: Harvard University Press, 1921], p. 169).

Is this what the gods really want? Lucian scoffs. Other philosophers also mocked aspects of pagan worship: The philosopher Heraclitus of Ephesus ridiculed those who worshipped images, suggesting that anyone who approaches and prays before statues as if they were gods acts like a person who tries to engage in conversation with houses (cited in Origen, *Contra Celsum* 1.5, translated by Henry Chadwick, [Cambridge: Cambridge University Press, 1953], p. 9). The Platonist teacher Celsus complains that even when images are made by craftsmen with loose morals, people still regard them as worth worshipping (ibid).

10. Cited by Eusebius, *The Preparation for the Gospel* 4.14d (translated by Edwin Hamilton Gifford [Grand Rapids, MI: Baker Book House, 1981], Part I, p. 167. Although Porphyry is writing after the *Gospel of Judas* was composed, the sentiment he expresses was widespread in the first and second centuries (see Attridge, op. cit.).

11. See *Natural History* 30.12, cited from Mary Beard, John North, and Simon Price, *Religions of Rome, Vol. 2: A Sourcebook*

(Cambridge: Cambridge University Press, 1998), pp. 156–160.

12. *Natural History* 30.12–13, For other examples of Romans offering human sacrifice, see Plutarch, *Roman Questions* 83, ibid; and the discussion of J. Rives, "Human Sacrifice among Pagans and Christians" in *The Journal of Roman Studies* 85 (1995), pp. 65–85.

13. Those hostile to Christians accused them of murdering and eating infants as a central "mystery" of their worship. One such critic is quoted as saying that initiates are required to kill a child, and then: "I can hardly mention this, but they thirstily lap up the infant's blood, eagerly tear his body apart, make a covenant over this sacrificial victim, and by complicity in the crime they bind themselves to mutual silence. These rites are more foul than any form of sacrilege" (Minucius Felix, *Octavius* 9.5, cited from Mary Beard, John North and Simon Price, *Religions of Rome. Vol. 2: A Sourcebook* [Cambridge: Cambridge University Press, 1998], p. 281).

How did such a slanderous charge of ritual murder and cannibalism get started? Some outsiders may have inferred this from what they heard about Christians eating "the flesh and blood" (bread and wine) of

God's son (see Stephen Benko, *Pagan Rome and the Early Christians* [Bloomington, IN: Indiana University Press, 1984], especially p. 62). But in any case, it fits the pattern we have seen of condemning other people's religious practices as impious and immoral (see J. Rives, "Human Sacrifice among Pagans and Christians" in *The Journal of Roman Studies* 85 [1995], pp. 65–85).

14. All references to this work are from Birger Pearson and Søren Giversen, *The Testimony of Truth,* pp. 101–203 in *Nag Hammadi Codices IX and X.* (Leiden: E. J. Brill, 1981).

15. See *Against Heresies* V.2.3; English translation from A. Clevelan Coxe, *The Ante-Nicene Fathers,* Vol. I (Grand Rapids, MI: Erdmans, 1885 [reprint 1979]), p. 528.

Chapter Four: The Mysteries of the Kingdom

1. See *Against Heresies* V.2.3.

2. For discussion, see Elaine Pagels, *The Gnostic Gospels* (New York: Random House, 1979), pp. 3–27, which indicates how this teaching also helped legitimize the structures of church authority that certain Christians were attempting to establish.

3. "For it is just that in that very creation in which they [the righteous] toiled or were

afflicted, being proved in every way by suffering, they should receive the reward of their suffering; and that in the creation in which they were slain because of their love to God, in that they should be revived again; and that in the creation in which they endured servitude, in that they should reign. For God is rich in all things, and all things are His. It is fitting, therefore, that the creation itself, being restored to its primeval condition, should without restraint be under the dominion of the righteous" (*Against Heresies,* V.32.1; ANF I, p. 561). Irenaeus then cites Paul, *Romans* 8:19–21 in support.

4. See Robinson and Smith, *The Nag Hammadi Library in English,* translated by James Brashier and Roger Bullard (Leiden: Brill Academic Publishers, 4th rev. ed., 1997), p. 377.

5. These two works were already known from a 1945 discovery near Nag Hammadi in Egypt, but the Tchacos Codex (TC) offers some significant variants (see the Coptic text edited by Rudolphe Kasser and Gregor Wurst, English translation by Marvin Meyer and F. Gaudard, notes by Marvin Meyer and Gregor Wurst). We would like to thank Marvin Meyer for generously allowing us to see an advance copy of the critical edition to be published by the

National Geographic Society, Washington, D.C.

6. *1 Apocalypse of James,* NHC 31:18–22 (translated by Douglas Parrott, in Robinson and Smith, *The Nag Hammadi Library in English,* p. 265).

7. *1 Apocalypse of James* TC 12:3–4.

8. *1 Apocalypse of James* NHC 30:1–6; TC 16:15–21.

9. *Letter of Peter to Philip,* NHC 137:21–30; TC 8:2–3.

10. Compare, for example, *Ephesians* 6:12: "Our struggle is not against enemies of blood and flesh, but against the rulers, against the authorities, against the cosmic powers of this present darkness, against the spiritual forces of evil in the heavenly places."

11. For more on the *Secret Revelation of John,* see Karen L. King, *The Secret Revelation of John* (Cambridge: Harvard University Press, 2005). All citations are from the English translation there.

12. Found in the *Acts of John* 94–96 (English translation in Edgar Hennecke and Wilhelm Schneemelcher, *New Testament Apocrypha, Vol. II Writings Relating to the Apostles, Apocalypses and Related Subjects*

(Louisville, KY: Westminster/John Knox Press, 1992), pp. 181–184.

A Final Note

1. For discussion of how these elements came to be included in the New Testament gospels, see, for example, Elaine Pagels, *The Origin of Satan* (New York: Random House, 1995).

ON THE TRANSLATION

1:8 Although the Coptic term translated here as "child" is a form of the word not otherwise known (ⲛϩⲣⲟⲧ, see Crum 631a, Bohairic; Kasser et al., op. cit. p. 20, n. 7), Antti Marjanen has suggested that the term here is a previously unknown Sahidic variant of the Bohairic (e-mail correspondence). The parallels given by Kasser et al., however, point to "child" (ⲡϣⲏⲣⲉ ϣⲏⲙ) or "youth" (ⲁⲗⲟⲩ). Note also the *Gospel of the Savior* 107:57–60, and references there by Charles Hedrick and Paul Mirecki, pp. 41, 103).

3:11 "not from this realm" following the restoration of Antti Marjanen and Ismo Dunderberg at 37:9: ϩⲛ [ⲡⲉⲓ]ⲁⲓ[ⲟⲛ ⲁⲛ ⲧ]ⲉ.

4:16 Following reconstruction of Iricinschi, Jenott, and Town-send: ⲑⲩⲥ [ⲓⲗⲥⲧⲏⲣⲓⲟⲛ], now also restored in the critical edition of Kasser and Wurst.

5:5 Read [ⲡⲁⲣⲭⲱⲛ ⲙⲡⲉⲭⲁ]ⲟⲥ (my restoration, tentative). The critical edition restores [ⲡⲁⲣⲭⲱⲛ ⲙ̄ⲡⲓⲕⲟⲥ]ⲙⲟⲥ ("the ruler of the world"); the final *m* is uncertain.

10:10 Restoration following Iricinschi, Jenott, and Townsend: ⲟ[ⲅⲁⲓⲱⲛ] ("a [realm]"). Rodolphe and Wurst, with a suggestion from John Turner, alternatively restore the passage: ⲙⲁⲣⲉϥϣⲱⲡ[ⲉ] ⲛ̄ϭⲓ ⲁ[ⲇⲁⲙⲁⲥ] ⲁⲩⲱ ⲁⲥϣⲱⲡⲉ [ⲛ̄ϭⲓ ⲧⲉⲡⲣⲟⲟⲇ]ⲟⲥ ("Let [Adamas] come into being and [the emanati]on came into being.") Let me suggest: ⲙⲁⲣⲉϥϣⲱⲡ[ⲉ] ⲛ̄ϭⲓ ⲁ[ⲇⲁⲙⲁⲥ] ⲁⲩⲱ ⲁⲥϣⲱⲡⲉ [ⲛ̄ϭⲓ ⲟⲩⲛⲉϥ]ⲟⲥ ("Let [Adamas] come into being and [a clou]d came into being.")

11:4 E.g., "according to the image of the angel" (sg.) or "the angels" (pl.); either reading fits the text.

15:12 The translation "place" follows the restoration of Iricinschi, Jenott, and Townsend: ⲧ[ⲟ]ⲡⲟⲥ.

ON THE COMMENTS ON THE TRANSLATION

1. See the very interesting examples given by Bart D. Ehrman, *The Orthodox Corrup*

272

tion of Scripture (Oxford: Oxford University Press, 1993).

2. See especially the work of Denise Kimber Buell, *Why This New Race: Ethnic Reasoning in Early Christianity* (New York: Columbia University Press, 2005).

3. See Michael A. Williams, *The Immovable Race: A Gnostic Designation and the Theme of Stability in Late Antiquity* (Leiden: Brill Academic Publishers, 1985), especially pp. 14–18, 26–27.

4. In the *Gospel of Mark,* Jesus repeatedly tries to keep his true identity secret, silencing not only the demons who know him but even his own disciples.

5. So, too, Levi in the *Gospel of Mary* accuses Peter of being on the side of their adversaries when he challenges the truth of Mary Magdalene's teaching (see *Mary* 10:8).

6. The crowds also do not understand that Jesus comes from God (*John* 7:33–34; 40–52).

7. For more discussion of this figure and Sethian views of the divine world, see Karen L. King, *The Secret Revelation of John* (Cambridge: Harvard University Press, 2005), pp. 85–88.

8. *1 Apocalypse of James* 40:22–26; see the discussion in Antti Marjanen, *The Woman Jesus Loved: Mary Magdalene in the*

Nag Hammadi Library and Related Documents (Leiden: Brill, 1996), pp. 122–146.

9. *1 Apocalypse of James* (TC) 27:25–28:5; 29:1–6.

10. For an excellent examination of views of same-sex relations in antiquity and Christianity, see Bernadette J. Brooten, *Love Between Women: Early Christian Responses to Female Homoeroticism* (Chicago: University of Chicago Press, 1996).

11. See *Phaedo* 66–69; 83d–84b; 84e–85b; quotation from 83d–e, *Plato,* Vol. I, translated by Harold North Fowler, Loeb Classical Library edition (Cambridge, MA: Harvard University Press, 1914), p. 291.

12. Plato, *Timaeus* 90a–b; *Plato,* Vol. IX, translated by R. G. Bury, Loeb Classical Library edition, (Cambridge, MA: Harvard University Press, 1929), p. 245, modified.

13. For an important recent study of the heavenly Temple and sacrificial practice, see Jonathan Klawans, *Purity, Sacrifice, and the Temple: Symbolism and Supersessionism in the Study of Ancient Judaism* (Oxford: Oxford University Press, 2006), especially pp. 111–174. The book examines how contemporary biases against sacrifice have distorted our views about the meaning of the Temple, purity law, and sacrifice among Jews and Christians in the ancient world. In particu-

lar, Klawans demonstrates that criticisms of the Temple cult, sacrifice, and "impure priests" did not necessarily entail complete rejection of those institutions and practices as such.

14. See George Johnson, "For the Anti-Evolutionists, Hope in High Places" (*New York Times* "Week in Review," Oct. 2, 2005), p. 4; Kenneth L. Woodward, "Evolution as Zero-Sum Game" (*New York Times,* Oct. 1, 2005), p. A29.

15. Cited in Johnson, "For the Evolutionists."

16. Johnson, ibid.

17. Many elements of the theology and cosmology of the *Gospel of Judas* are similar to a set of newly discovered writings found in Egypt that scholars classify as "Sethian Gnosticism" or simply "Sethianism." One of these is *The Secret Revelation of John,* with which several scholars have compared the *Gospel of Judas,* notably Marvin Meyer ("Judas and the Gnostic Connection" in Kasser, Meyer, and Wurst, editors, *The Gospel of Judas,* op. cit. Not only are there important similarities, crucial differences also appear. For example, in *The Secret Revelation of John,* the true God is not responsible for appointing the lower beings who shape the material world, but rather

against God's will, the world comes into being at the hand of an ignorant and arrogant pretender god. An extensive episode tells of how this happens when a divine being, named Sophia ("Wisdom") acts without the permission of the Invisible Spirit and her male consort, thus setting in motion the creation of the lower world and the enslavement of humanity to its wicked rulers. For more on these topics, see Karen L. King, *The Secret Revelation of John,* op. cit.; for more on Sethianism, see Karen L. King, *What Is Gnosticism?,* pp. 154–169.

18. See, for example, *The Secret Revelation of John* 7:1–25 (BG 29:18–32; NHC II 6:10–11:2).

19. Other new early Christian writings in the Nag Hammadi Codices and the Berlin Codex, especially *Eugnostos the Blessed* and its parallel text, the *Sophia of Jesus Christ,* also rely on similar numbers to describe the orderliness of the universe as a creation of God. These works explicitly state that the model for the number of the zodiac, the seasons, and the days is found in the divine realm above. Similarly the *Gospel of the Egyptians* 56:22–58:23 tells of the creation of the angels who rule the lower world, including Saklas, Nebruel, and others known to the author of the *Gospel of Judas.*

20. See, for example, a treatise called the *Epinomis* (which ancients wrongly attributed to Plato) that argued that life and death are controlled by number, and since the heavenly bodies teach humanity about numbers, the study of astronomy is essential to attain wisdom and piety.

21. *Epinomis* 978A, Loeb Classical Library edition. As David Sedley puts it, referring to Plato (*Timaeus* 90c–d): "(A)stronomy is the privileged route to human understanding, since by discovering the mathematical laws underlying the revolutions of the heaven it makes our rational soul share the thought patterns of the worlds' divine soul" (" 'Becoming like god' in the *Timaeus* and Aristotle," in *Interpreting the Timaeus-Critias: Proceedings of the IV Symposium Platonicum Selected Papers.* Tomás Calvo and Luc Brisson, editors [Sankt Augstin: Academia Verlag, 1997]), p. 332.

22. Plutarch, *Nicias* 23, cited from Alan Scott, *Origen and the Life of the Stars: A History of an Idea* (Oxford: Clarendon Press, 1991), p. 6.

23. Scott, *Origen and the Life of the Stars,* op. cit., p. 16, referring to *Laws* 889b–c. According to Scott, Plato countered this charge by arguing that "the movements of heaven corresponded to mathematical law"

of numbers, offering the strongest proof for the existence of God as the mind that controls the heavens through the working of the living soul. "The perfectly ordered movements of the stars proves the existence of the supreme soul which directs them" (ibid).

24. See star of the Magi (*Matthew* 2:1–12); eclipse at death of Christ (*Matthew* 27:45; *Mark* 25:33; *Luke* 23:44); celestial signs to announce Christ's return (*Matthew* 24:29; *Mark* 13:24–25; *Luke* 21:25). Yet whatever assumptions about the effectiveness of astrology, the practice came to be thoroughly condemned, and this is the position still used to describe early Christian attitudes; see Everett Ferguson, "Astrology," in *Encyclopedia of Early Christianity*. Second ed. (New York: Garland Publishing, 1998), pp. 136–137. Tamsyn S. Barton argues that once the power of the church was established, it worked to undermine astrology, which threatened the church's authority. See a brief history of the attitudes toward astrology by Christians in the first centuries in Barton, *Power and Knowledge: Astrology, Physiognomics, and Medicine under the Roman Empire* (Ann Arbor: University of Michigan Press, 1994), pp. 62–69, and *Ancient Astrology* (London: Routledge, 1994),

pp. 64–85.

25. Scott, *Origen and the Life of the Stars,* op. cit., p. 145, referring to *Philocalia* 23.1, 2; *In Jeremias* fragment 49.

26. All translations and references to *I Enoch* are from *The Old Testament Pseudepigrapha: Apocalyptic Literature and Testaments,* James H. Charlesworth, editor (Garden City, NY: Doubleday, 1983), pp. 5–89.

27. See Plato, *Timaeus* 27d–30b; 37d; 41c–42e, in *Plato,* translated by R. G. Bury, Vol. IX, Loeb Classical Library (Cambridge, MA: Harvard University Press, 1929).

28. See the extended discussion of Bruce J. Malina, *On the Genre and Message of Revelation: Star Visions and Sky Journeys* (Peabody, MA: Hendrickson Publishers, 1995).

29. This reading is based on the excellent insight of Stephen Emmel (from an unpublished paper on "The Presuppositions and the Purpose of the *Gospel of Judas,*" presented at the "Colloque international, CNRS-Université Paris IV-Sorbonne," titled *"L'Évangile de Judas. Le contexte historique et littéraire d'un nouvel apocryphe,"* October 27–28, 2006, the proceedings of which are expected to be published under the editorship of Madeleine Scopello). My thanks to

him for generously making his paper available in advance of publication.

30. See, for example, the excellent study of François Bovon, *The Last Days of Jesus* (Louisville, KY: Westminster/John Knox Press, 2006), a readable introduction to New Testament scholarship on the last days of Jesus that charts a middle path between "history remembered" and "prophecy historicized," arguing that both are part of Christian attempts to understand the theological meaning of Jesus's death, and pointing out where Christian tellings of this story are motivated by anti-Jewish sentiment.

ACKNOWLEDGMENTS

Reading Judas is a joint effort, the product of many delightful discussions and shared labors. It is our first attempt to make sense of this difficult and exciting new work, and we have no doubt that scholars and readers will continue to add to our understanding of this remarkable work for years to come.

In the process of writing this work, we have received help from many people. In particular we would like to thank Antti Marjanen for his expert conversation about problems in the Coptic text of the *Gospel of Judas.* Our special thanks as well to Edwin Iricinschi, Lance Jenott, and Philippa Townsend, who generously shared their lovely English translation with us. Marvin Meyer provided an advance copy of the critical edition of the Tchacos Codex, for which we are very grateful. Stephen Emmel allowed us to read and cite his excellent essay on the conclusion to the *Gospel of Judas*

— our sincerest thanks. Our thanks to Sarah Coakley for supplying helpful bibliography on atonement theology. Warmest gratitude goes to Hal Taussig for his continued friendship, support, and good advice. We are especially grateful to our friend and colleague James Cone for invaluable conversations and encouragement.

The timely production of *Reading Judas* also owes much to the long hours of careful work by the staff at Viking. In particular, our thanks for the outstanding editorial work of Clifford Corcoran; for the careful correction of many manuscript infelicities by Veronica Windholz with the help of Noirin Lucas, Jane Cavolina, and Gabriel De Vries; for the handsome design work of Francesca Belanger on the text and Jasmine Lee's creation of a beautiful jacket design; for the timely production work of Grace Veras and Fabiana Van Arsdell; for the outstanding marketing efforts of Nancy Sheppard, Carolyn Coleburn, and Ben Petrone; and thanks to Tory Klose for masterminding the whole operation.

Our deepest gratitude belongs to our intrepid editor, Wendy Wolf, who encouraged us throughout and whose calm energy and insight steered our first thoughts into a completed work. Her insight, experience, and undaunted optimism not only helped us through, but made the process much more enjoyable.

— Elaine Pagels and Karen L. King

These acknowledgments could not be complete without expressing gratitude to Eric Wanner, president of the Russell Sage Foundation, and to the dedicated members of his wonderful staff, for the opportunity to complete this work among the scholars currently at the Foundation this year. And finally, my deepest thanks to Sarah and Dave Pagels for their steadfast love and encouragement throughout the writing of this book and to Kent Greenawalt and members of the Greenawalt family for their continuing kindness and support.

— Elaine Pagels

I would like to give a special word of acknowledgment and thanks to the wonderful people who make up the open and welcoming community of my parish, Church of Our Savior in Arlington, Massachusetts. More than you know, your commitment to a common spiritual journey, to nurturing the presence of God in all of life, to exploring faith with openness to difference and change, with creativity, compassion, and laughter, have been a major support for my work. My deepest gratitude.

— Karen L. King!

ABOUT THE AUTHORS

Karen L. King is Winn Professor of Ecclesiastical History at the Harvard Divinity School and author of four books, including *The Gospel of Mary of Magdala* and *What is Gnosticism?* She lives in Cambridge, Massachusetts.

Elaine Pagels is Harrington Spear Paine Professor of Religion at Princeton University and the author of six previous books including *The Gnostic Gospels* (winner of the National Book Critics Circle Award and the National Book Award), and the *New York Times* bestseller *Beyond Belief.* She lives in Princeton, New Jersey.